The Instructional Leader's Guide to Informal Classroom Observations

Second Edition

Sally J. Zepeda

EYE ON EDUCATION
6 DEPOT WAY WEST, SUITE 106
LARCHMONT, NY 10538
(914) 833–0551
(914) 833–0761 fax www.eyeoneducation.com

Library of Congress Cataloging-in-Publication Data

Zepeda, Sally J., 1956-
  The instructional leader's guide to informal classroom observations / Sally J. Zepeda.—2nd ed.
     p. cm.
   ISBN 978-1-59667-091-4
   1. Observation (Educational method) 2. School principals—United States. 3. Teacher-principal relationships—United States. 4. School supervision—United States. I. Title.
   LB1731.6.Z46 2008
   370.71'1—dc22

                                                                    2008026425

10 9 8 7 6 5 4 3 2 1

Editorial and production services provided by
Hypertext Book and Journal Services
738 Saltillo St., San Antonio, TX 78207-6953 (210-227-6055)

Acknowledgments

The professionals who reviewed this manuscript shared their perspectives selflessly, making this book stronger because of their insights. I am indebted to these professionals—Richard A. Flanary, Director of National Association of Secondary School Principals's Department of Professional Development Services; Laura McCullough, Director of Instructional Services, Waynesboro School District, Virginia; and Todd Wiedemann, Principal, Berrien Springs High School, Michigan.

There are always people who work behind the scenes while a book is being written. A special acknowledgment goes to Kevin Shorner-Johnson, Oksana Parylo, Deb Teitelbaum, and Ed Bengtson, research assistants in the Department of Lifelong Education, Administration, and Policy at the University of Georgia. Kevin, Oksana, Deb, and Ed provided invaluable assistance proofreading and helping me to meet deadlines. Bob Sickles challenged and encouraged me to write this book after I "gritched" about the lost art of informal classroom observation as it was envisioned many years ago. He fueled the fire for me to write the first edition and again for me to get the second edition out after our discussion of how these tools and techniques are being used in the field by school personnel. Frank Aguirre of Hypertext Book and Journal Services played an instrumental role in making forms and tools in this book "user-friendly."

This second edition includes an expanded set of classroom observation tools, moving from 23 to 40 and more linkages to the job-embedded nature of the informal classroom observations. There is a new chapter about how principals and teachers can extend learning opportunities by examining student work and other artifacts in postobservation conversations. These additions made sense based on feedback from the field of practice. I am indebted to the professionals who have shared insights about how they used the tools in the first edition of the book.

About the Author

Sally J. Zepeda served as a high school teacher and administrator in K-12 schools before entering higher education. She is a professor in the Department of Lifelong Education, Administration, and Policy in the Program of Educational Administration and Policy at the University of Georgia, where she teaches courses in instructional supervision, professional development, teacher evaluation, and school improvement.

Sally has written widely about instructional leadership and the supervision and evaluation of teaching. She edited a special issue of the *NASSP Bulletin* on instructional supervision for the National Association of Secondary School Principals. In 2005, Sally was named a Master Professor by the University Council of Educational Administration. In 2008, Sally received the Johnnye V. Cox Award from the University of Georgia, College of Education's Educational Administration and Policy Program. The award recognizes an individual for significant contributions in supervision and leadership.

Sally's 15 books include such titles as *Professional Development: What Works; Instructional Leadership for School Improvement; The Principal as Instructional Leader: A Handbook for Supervisors* (2nd ed.); *and Instructional Supervision: Applying Tools and Concepts* (2nd ed.).

Free Downloads

The 40 Classroom Observation tools discussed and displayed in this book are also available on Eye On Education's Web site as Adobe Acrobat PDF files. Those who have purchased this book have permission to download them and print them out. You can access these downloads by visiting Eye On Education's Web site: www.eyeoneducation.com.

Click on FREE Downloads or search or browse our Web site to find this book and then scroll down for downloading instructions.

You'll need your book-buyer access code: **OBS-7091-4**

Classroom Observation Tools

Table of Contents

1
Readying for Informal Classroom Observations

In This Chapter ...

- ♦ Why informal classroom observations are important
- ♦ Principals make the commitment to get out and about
- ♦ Principals know their people
- ♦ Principals assess the context of supervision and their own beliefs
- ♦ Principals develop the leadership skills of the administrative team
- ♦ Principals develop practices to track the observation efforts of the administrative team

A resounding finding in the literature of the accountability movement is that teacher quality improves student learning. If this premise is true, then the assessment of teaching in classrooms needs to become the first step toward improving instruction and assisting teachers to examine their practices. Assisting teachers begins at the place where instruction occurs—in the classroom. Principals and other school leaders are urged to remember that, like students, teachers need opportunities to grow, develop, and learn.

What Is This Book About?

This book focuses on assisting the principal (and others) as he or she works with teachers in formative ways, primarily through informal classroom observations. To make informal classroom observations a priority, principals must frame their work habits and daily routines around dropping by classrooms and then following up by providing teachers with feedback and opportunities for reflection and inquiry. This book is written for the principal who wants to be viewed by teachers as a support for the instructional program. Assistant principals, department chairs, lead teachers, teacher leaders, and others can enhance the instructional program by developing a better understanding of informal classroom observations.

This book provides a series of classroom observation tools to help frame the informal classroom observation and follow-up discussion with teachers. This second edition includes additional classroom observation tools that have been field tested by school personnel. There is also a new chapter with tips and cues on how to incorporate examining student work and other artifacts in postobservation conversations.

Professionals are encouraged to use and adapt the tools in this book. The value of the tools and techniques offered is that they are easily adaptable. Principals, assistant principals, and coaches need not think that they have to use every tool to be an effective instructional leader. Pick the tools that make sense and use the existing tools to develop more tools.

These tools are available to you in three different ways. In each chapter you'll see how the tools can be implemented by an instructional leader during classroom observations and in postobservation conferences. In the Appendix, you will find a blank version of the same tools that appear throughout the chapters of the book. Permission is granted to those who have purchased this book to photocopy the blank forms and use them while working with teachers. Blank versions of the tools can also be downloaded from Eye On Education's Web site: www.eyeoneducation.com. See page v for details.

WHY INFORMAL CLASSROOM OBSERVATIONS ARE IMPORTANT

Informal classroom observation is a way to get instructional supervision and teacher evaluation out of the main office. Teachers need feedback more than once or twice a year. Informal classroom observations provide valuable opportunities for more frequent interaction between the supervisor and the teacher. Informal classroom observations can provide opportunities to extend the talk about teaching if the principal carves out enough time after an informal classroom observation to engage teachers in a discussion of their instructional practices.

Recently, informal classroom observations have become vogue with principals who are learning the art and science of the "3-minute walk-through" advocated by the research, practice, and work of Downey, Steffy, English, Frase, and Poston (2004). The value of the 3-minute walk-through is acknowledged. This book, however, offers a different view of informal classroom observations. Namely, the informal classroom observation should be extended to more than 3 minutes to achieve its purposes—working with teachers in ways that are more meaningful. A 3-minute walk-through is simply not enough time to capture a sustained picture of teaching and learning, and that is why this book advocates a more enlarged view of the informal classroom observation. In general, teachers want context-specific information about their teaching, and data observed in the window of a 15- to 20-minute observation can provide such opportunities for specific feedback, discussion, and reflection.

Figure 1.1. Strengths of Job-Embedded Learning

Job-embedded learning …
- ♦ does not require participants to set aside a separate time to learn;
- ♦ promotes immediate application of what is learned;
- ♦ can be formal or informal;
- ♦ links current information to previously learned information; and
- ♦ supports the generation of new ideas.

Teaching and Learning to Teach Are Complex

Part of the process of learning to teach occurs in the overall school context and in the varying contexts of classrooms where instruction unfolds in the presence of children. Learning to teach is mediated through such variables as preparation route (traditional or alternative certification), experience, professional development opportunities, and so on.

Informal Teacher Observations Support Job-Embedded Learning

Informal teacher observations and follow-up postobservation conferences are important job-embedded learning strategies because principals and teachers can purposefully learn from "their work activities" (Wood & Killian, 1998, p. 52). The strengths of job-embedded learning are detailed in Figure 1.1.

Through classroom observations, teachers and principals can link "learning and real-life problems" (Sparks & Hirsh, 1997, p. 52). As a job-embedded approach, informal classroom observations embrace what we know about attributes of job-embedded learning:

1. adds relevance for teacher learning;
2. feedback is built into the process; and
3. facilitates the transfer of new skills into practice (Zepeda, 2008).

Job-Embedded Learning Is More Relevant

First, because job-embedded learning is a part of the teacher's daily work, it is, by its very nature, relevant to the learner. Job-embedded learning addresses goals and concerns of the individual teacher. In addition, job-embedded learning occurs at the teacher's job site. Therefore, the teacher's learning becomes an integral part of the culture of the classroom and by extension the school.

Feedback is Built Into the Process of Job-Embedded Learning

Second, through informal observations, feedback is built in through the structure of the postobservation conference. The data collected during the classroom observation creates fertile ground for ongoing discussions about teaching and learning. Teachers can use data to help them see their classroom practices better; if informal classroom observations occur regularly during the course of a year, data can accumulate and teachers can begin to use this data to chronicle implementation of new instructional skills, to provide artifacts for assessing transition from one learning activity to the next, or to use to frame future classroom practices.

Job-Embedded Learning Facilitates the Transfer of New Skills Into Practice

Third, job-embedded learning facilitates the transfer of new skills into practice. When ongoing support is linked with the lessons learned from classroom observations and time is afforded within the regular school day for teachers to make informed decisions based on data, transfer of skills into practice becomes part of the job.

The research on job-embedded learning reports that it

- enhances reflection;
- promotes collegiality;
- combats isolation;
- makes learning more relevant to each teacher;
- increases transfer of newly learned skills;
- supports the ongoing refinement of practice; and
- fosters a common lexicon that facilitates dialogue and improvement.

Teachers learn to teach on the job through their experiences as they plan for instruction and interact with their students. When teachers have the opportunity to talk about teaching, to share their insights with someone else, and to reflect on what occurs in the classroom, their learning increases. This type of job-embedded learning is enhanced through the efforts of the observant principal who facilitates opportunities for teachers to reflect and refine their practices through sustained feedback based on data from informal classroom observations.

PRINCIPALS MAKE THE COMMITMENT TO GET OUT AND ABOUT

The overall intent of instructional supervision is teacher growth and development. Effective supervisors do not wait to be invited into classrooms; they find opportunities for informal visits, in addition to the more formal, mandated classroom observations tied to evaluation. They constantly scan the learning environment for ways to help teachers improve on their talents.

Principals who find time to drop by classrooms seek and value opportunities to connect with their teachers, and they have a sincere desire to see teachers succeed as they face classroom challenges. Based on what principals observe in classrooms over time, they are able to:

♦ extend the talk about teaching and learning;

♦ make purposeful efforts to promote whole-school involvement by sharing what others have learned;

♦ involve others in conducting informal classroom observations, including members of the administrative team, department chairs, and teachers;

♦ get creative about sharing what has been learned through faculty newsletters, electronic mailing lists, and video clips with promising teaching practices, and

♦ embed learning and professional development opportunities within the reality of the school's context.

With a commitment to making informal classroom observations a part of the workday, these goals are achievable. The principal must wrap his or her thinking around the context of the school and the characteristics of the teachers in the building and then carve out time in an already busy and hectic workday. Effective leaders "know their people."

PRINCIPALS KNOW THEIR PEOPLE

Effective leaders do their homework up front, even before conducting their first informal classroom observation. These leaders know their people, in part, because they do several things:

♦ assess the characteristics of teachers;

♦ recognize teachers' career stages;

♦ assess teachers' willingness to learn; and

♦ know, honor, and respect the adult learner.

Assessing the Characteristics of Teachers

Tool 1 will assist principals in broadly profiling any given faculty. By gathering statistical information about a school's faculty, the principal can begin to reflect about teachers' learning needs. It might be useful to have a faculty roster and a seniority list (typically available from the district office) to help track and tally information.

Tool 1: Assessing the Broad Characteristics of a Faculty

1. Number of teachers = **103**   Male = **42** Female = **61**

2. For each teacher, tally the number of years in teaching.
   Total number of years of experience = **900**
   Average years of faculty experience = **9**

3. Number of teachers whose experience falls within the following service ranges:
   a. 1–3 years = **23**
   b. 4–7 years = **45**
   c. 8–11 years = **0**
   d. 12–15 years = **15**
   e. 16–19 years = **0**
   f. 20+ years = **20**

4. Number of first-year teachers = **11**

5. Number of teachers who will retire at the end of the year = **19**

6. Wildcards:
   First-year teachers with experience = **0**
   Alternatively certified teachers = **5**
   Teachers returning to work after an extended leave = **2**
   Other = **0**

7. What overall patterns do you notice?
   About 20% of these teachers have three or fewer years of experience.
   About half of the teachers are at the midpoint of their careers.
   About 20% of the teachers are in the wind-down stage of their careers.
   About 18% of the teachers are going to retire at the end of the current school year; more than likely there will be an influx of less experienced teachers hired the following year.

To extend the contextual information about the broad characteristics of teachers in the building, the principal next examines teacher career stages.

Recognizing Teachers' Career Stages

Regardless of experience, position, grade level, or subject area, learning to teach is a process that continues throughout one's career, and this is why instructional supervision is important. As adults, teachers have learning needs that shift over time, signaling inexact stages of development. At one time, most teachers entered the profession immediately following a 4-year preparation program. Now, many teachers having had successful careers in other areas enter the profession through alternative certification routes. Suffice it to say, knowledge about teachers' career stages is important if principals are going to work more effectively to improve instructional support through the informal classroom observation process.

Figure 1.2 provides an inexact but useful way of thinking about teachers' career stages. The types of professional supports that teachers need at the beginning of their careers are very different from those needed by teachers who are further along in their careers.

Figure 1.2. Teachers' Career Stages and Developmental Needs

Stage	Name	Years in Field (Approximate)	Developmental Theory and Needs
1	Preservice	0	Training and preparation for a profession
2	Induction	1–2	Survival stage: Seeks safety and desires to learn the day-to-day operations of the school and the complexities of facing new situations in the classroom
3	Competency	3–5	Confidence in work mounts, as does understanding of the multifaceted role of teaching
4	Enthusiasm	5–8	Actively seeks professional development and other opportunities; high job satisfaction
5	Career frustration	Varies	Teacher burnout
6	Stability	Varies	Complacency; innovation is low
7	Career wind down	Varies	Coasts on past laurels and status; little effort
8	Career exit	Varies	End of teaching career

Sources: Adapted from Burden (1982); Burke, Christensen, and Fessler (1984); Christensen, Burke, Fessler, and Hagstrom (1983); Feiman and Floden (1980); Huberman, 1993; Katz, 1972.

Through an educator's career span, Burden (1982, pp. 1–2) found that many changes occur in the following areas:

♦ job skills, knowledge, and behaviors—in areas such as teaching methods, discipline strategies, and curriculum planning;

♦ attitudes and outlooks—in areas such as images of teaching, professional confidence and maturity, and willingness to try new teaching methods and concerns; and

♦ job events—in areas such as changes in grade level, school, or district; involvement in additional professional responsibilities; and age of entry and retirement.

Given this range, it is logical for principals to use informal classroom observation as a tool to assist teachers with the uncertainties they face as a result of these changes. These changes also can affect teachers' willingness to learn.

Assessing Teachers' Willingness to Learn

People learn at their own pace. Workplace conditions, such as the relationship between administration and teachers and the norms of collegiality, also affect learning. Learning can neither be mandated nor imposed. Adults respond to learning opportunities differently. Just as effective teachers know when to shift instruction and learning activities to meet the individual and collective needs of students, principals can be more effective if they know their teachers as "learners." From this perspective, the principal is encouraged to view the school as a classroom in which all members are engaged in learning individually and collectively. The principal is able to assess current practices by examining the following:

♦ Learning: Do teachers seek out learning opportunities offered at the site, district, or externally, such as, graduate school, local and national conferences, and workshops?

♦ Sharing: Do teachers share their knowledge and expertise with other teachers? Do teachers meet to share what they have learned in professional development activities?

♦ Reflecting and discussing: Do teachers openly discuss what they have learned about their own teaching practices?

♦ Examining the talk over time: Are discussions held over sustained periods? One-time discussions do little to promote professional growth; continual discussion about progress and setbacks promotes personal and professional development.

♦ Reading the word: Are books, professional journals, and technology used as resources? Are these resources readily available and shared?

After examining these conditions, principals can further ready themselves for conducting informal classroom observations by understanding teachers as adult learners.

Knowing, Honoring, and Respecting the Adult Learner

Although this book is limited in its coverage of the principles of adult learning, there are several assumptions about adult learning that serve as a baseline for helping principals work more effectively with teachers.

The principal who promotes adult development strives to make learning experiences

♦ self-directed, with the learner at the center of all activities;

♦ collaborative;

♦ promoting of trust, reflection, and open exchanges; and

♦ ongoing and sustained (Brookfield, 1986; Knowles, 1980).

Getting out of the office and entering the classroom to observe teachers is an important way to honor teachers' work and to help them to grow as adult learners. The principal who becomes a welcome guest in the classroom does so not by directing or being critical of the teacher, but by forming a partnership with the teacher. The value of the principal getting out and about lies in the opportunity to provide teachers with occasions to reflect on their classroom practices through the objective data collected in informal observations. The power that results from this feedback and the dialogue it encourages will be examined in later chapters.

PRINCIPALS ASSESS THE CONTEXT OF SUPERVISION AND THEIR OWN BELIEFS

Teachers want accessible, visible principals, but they do not want simple open-door policies or mobile principals in the halls during passing periods. Teachers want principals to visit them in their classrooms, and they desire constructive feedback. Assessment of the context of supervision includes understanding the history of supervision and evaluation, knowing the intent and purpose of supervision and evaluation, and reflecting on the interactions, past and present, between teachers and the principal. These factors shape the environment in which supervision evolves.

To create the conditions for effective informal classroom observations, the principal needs to reflect on the nature of the interactions that surround supervisory practices. The principal can assess the nature of prior classroom observations by asking, answering, and then reflecting on the meanings that his or her responses hold for the following questions:

- ♦ Are teachers used to seeing me and other administrators in their classrooms beyond the mandated classroom observations used to evaluate?

- ♦ Do I merely report what I observe?

- ♦ Do I try to link other activities, such as professional development, to the supervisory process?

- ♦ Are postobservation conferences conducted in a timely manner?

- ♦ Where are pre- and postobservation conferences conducted? (In the teacher's classroom? The main office?)

Learning and refining existing supervisory skills are ongoing practices that continually evolve as one gains experience and nurtures working relationships with teachers.

The principal often works with other site administrators and teacher leaders who should be a part of the supervisory efforts. The principal is encouraged to spend time nurturing administrative team members.

PRINCIPALS DEVELOP THE LEADERSHIP SKILLS OF THE ADMINISTRATIVE TEAM

Given the size of many schools, it is almost impossible to expect the principal to stand alone, conducting all informal classroom observations. While there is no substitute for the principal's visible presence in classrooms, there is a need for the administrative team to be engaged in the work of informal classroom observations. This involvement will multiply efforts, and, by including members of the administrative team, the principal creates important conditions to do the following:

- ♦ promote dialogue;
- ♦ affirm teachers' strengths;
- ♦ assist teachers in identifying areas of instruction needing improvement;
- ♦ target areas for professional development; and
- ♦ encourage reflection.

Before this can take place, however, members of the administrative team need to be informed and prepared to take on this responsibility. A solid beginning point is to understand the beliefs, values, and assumptions that the administrative team holds regarding teaching, learning, and the efforts needed to support teachers through informal classroom observations. These understandings are important because an administrative team that operates with similar beliefs, values, and assumptions sends a unified and powerful message to teachers.

As the leader, the principal is encouraged to set aside time for sustained discussion so that administrative team members can collectively explore their responses to the following open-ended statements:

- ♦ As a team, we plan for …
- ♦ As a team, we monitor …
- ♦ As a team, we model …
- ♦ As a team, we recognize and celebrate …
- ♦ As a team, we will are willing to confront …
- ♦ As a team, we believe effective teachers are those who …
- ♦ As a team, we believe an effective classroom is one in which …
- ♦ As a team, we believe teachers grow professionally by …
- ♦ As a team, we support teaching and learning by …

Without such introspection, the school's administrative team will not be synchronized to work alongside the principal to meet the needs of teachers. An administrative team that works together can do the following:

- ♦ build a unified vision for supervision and professional development;
- ♦ create a healthy learning culture;
- ♦ serve as valuable resources to help teachers meet their needs;
- ♦ coordinate and provide appropriate learning opportunities based on these needs; and
- ♦ grow as professionals from their work in the school.

Making informal classroom observations an administrative priority takes concerted effort on the part of the principal and the administrative team. It takes time to make informal classroom observations a habit of mind and practice. Such a commitment is really a commitment to the overall improvement of the instructional program that focuses on the efforts of teachers but is dependent, in part, on the following tasks of the administrative team:

- ♦ *Redefining relationships with each other and with teachers.* This process begins with the principal flattening the hierarchical structures within leadership teams (e.g., principal, associate principal, assistant principal, deans, instructional deans, department chairs, lead teachers, and grade-level coordinators).
- ♦ *Sharing responsibility for learning.* All team members need to assume an active role in providing learning opportunities for themselves as they work with teachers.

- *Creating an atmosphere of interdependence.* Each member of the team needs to feel a sense of belonging, contributing to individual and collective learning opportunities while working alongside fellow administrative team members and teachers.

- *Making time for professional development.* Time is often cited as the main reason why principals and other members of the administrative team cannot function as instructional leaders. Consider the reaction teachers might receive if they indicated that they did not have time to make it to class or correct student work.

- *Developing a plan for professional development, with teacher needs guiding the process.* No plan that is not grounded in the needs of its learners will yield significant results.

- *Rotating responsibilities.* Rotation of specific duties and responsibilities associated with professional development can help to get all members of the administrative team on the same proverbial page. This rotation also can assist with breaking down barriers between people within the organization while supporting the development of skills and expertise for all team members.

- *Linking schoolwide initiatives.* The coordination of school initiatives will reduce unnecessary duplication of programs and provide resources to support initiatives.

PRINCIPALS DEVELOP PRACTICES TO TRACK THE OBSERVATION EFFORTS OF THE ADMINISTRATIVE TEAM

Informal observations should be tracked. Tool 2 (see page 13) provides an example of how principals can track the informal classroom observations made by administrative team members.

By reviewing the record of formal and informal classroom observations, principals can determine whether any teachers were missed, whether observations were spread evenly throughout the day (indicated by the period or time of the observation) as well as the year, what follow-up topics were discussed, and when the postobservation conferences occurred. Principals also can look for patterns. For example, in Tool 2, Marlowe did not observe Baker for 4 months, and there was a nearly 2-week delay in the follow-up; Linton balanced informal and informal observations, and Burton did not engage Schmidt in any follow-up to the informal classroom observations. The principal should interpret these patterns in the context of the school and the characteristics of the teachers being supervised.

Tool 2. Tracking Informal Observations

Teacher	Observer	Informal Observations	Date of Follow-Up	Formal Observations	Period(s)/ Time(s)	Follow-up Topics
Adams	Schmidt	9/04/2008 11/03/2008	9/05/2008 11/04/2008	10/06/2008	1 (8:15-8:30) 5 (11:10-11:20)	Cooperative learning grouping
Baker	Marlowe	11/07/2008	11/10/2008	3/20/2008	1 (8:15-8:25) 1 (8:15-8:25)	Instructional pacing
Beatty	Linton	9/05/2008 9/08/2008 10/20/2008 11/12/2008	9/08/2008 9/08/2008 10/21/2008 11/14/2008	10/07/2008 10/14/2008 11/03/2008 11/26/2008	1 (8:30-8:45) 3 (10:10-10:25) 1 (8:15-8:25) 6 (1:05-1:15)	Classroom management; beginning- and end-of-period procedures
Burton	Schmidt	9/08/2008 11/20/2008	None None	10/31/2005	1 (8:00-8:15) 8 (2:15-2:30)	Classroom management

Looking Ahead ...

The next chapter details the intent of informal classroom observations, the premise behind informal classroom observations, and some basic guidelines to consider.

2

Framing Informal Classroom Observations

In This Chapter...

♦ The intent of teacher observation and instructional supervision
♦ Informal classroom observations
♦ Link informal classroom observations to schoolwide instructional improvement efforts
♦ Guidelines for informal classroom observations

To endure, a supervisory program that includes informal classroom observations that go beyond hit and miss requires an understanding of the intents of teacher observation and supervision. Informal classroom observations need to be based on guidelines to bolster teacher learning and development, and they should not be viewed or conducted as a "drive-through" in which a principal blitzes in and out of the classroom without offering some type of feedback. The drive-through approach just does not give the principal enough time to capture the events of the classroom, to collect data that are stable, or to provide enough hooks to engage the teacher in reflective dialogue.

THE INTENT OF TEACHER OBSERVATION AND INSTRUCTIONAL SUPERVISION

Observing teachers in action is the primary way of assessing teaching. Through formal and informal classroom observations, principals gain insights into classroom practices: instructional strategies, learning activities (including performance assessments), the taught curriculum, and the types of teacher and student interactions that evolve throughout the course of instruction. Effective classroom observations support the overall instructional program and the teachers who deliver it. Classroom observations also signal to teachers that the principal cares about them and the work they do. The principal's classroom presence promotes a healthy climate and creates conditions for the ongoing discussion, reflection, and refinement of practices.

Both Teachers and Principals Benefit From Classroom Observations

Classroom observations, whether they are formal or informal, provide opportunities for both the principal and the teacher to develop a broader range of understanding of the complexities of teaching and learning. For this range of understanding to emerge, classroom observations must occur over time with sustained attention to the processes used to observe teachers (observation tools are examined in chapter 4). Classroom observations provide opportunities *for teachers* to do the following:

- ◆ learn more about their teaching through the principal's support and presence;
- ◆ extend talk about teaching and reduce feelings of isolation;
- ◆ examine what works well and which areas of instruction or class-room management could be enhanced by modifying practice;
- ◆ receive affirmation of their instructional efforts; and
- ◆ gauge short- and long-term efforts by examining objective data collected over a sustained period of time.

For principals, there are benefits and opportunities as well. Principals benefit from informal observations because they

- ◆ learn more about teaching and learning;
- ◆ share alternative strategies observed in other classrooms with teachers;
- ◆ frame professional development opportunities for teachers across grade levels and subject areas;
- ◆ obtain a deeper understanding of the complexities of the classroom and how teachers handle these complexities;
- ◆ lend assistance to teachers who have needs;
- ◆ gain more than snapshot views of teachers; and
- ◆ enhance the supervisory and evaluation plan at the site.

The intent of supervision is to improve teaching and to lend assistance to teachers as they move throughout their careers. To this end, supervision is a proactive, ongoing set of processes and procedures.

INFORMAL CLASSROOM OBSERVATIONS

Every school system has processes in place for formal teacher evaluations that are based on state statutes regarding evaluation, union agreements, and other context-specific factors that make each school system unique. It is wise to know system-wide policies and procedures, along with the history of supervision at the site. Notwithstanding, the way that informal observations are conducted will dictate teachers' willingness to embrace this practice as an ongoing component of professional learning.

Management by Wandering Around

Informal classroom observation has evolved in the literature and in practice. Recently, there has been resurgence in attention to informal classroom observation. The popularity of informal classroom observation can be tied to the *management by wandering around* (MBWA) movement, popularized by Peters and Waterman (1982) in their book *In Search of Excellence: Lessons From America's Best Run Companies.*

Executives who embraced MBWA promoted informal communication and personal involvement with employees by getting out of the office. Through this accessibility and visibility, executives were able to ensure accountability and affirm the work of employees. The practice of informal classroom observations also embraces getting supervision and evaluation out of the main office, situating principals as active participants in the instructional lives of their teachers by promoting visibility and accessibility.

Walking-Around Supervision and Short Visits

In the supervision and teacher evaluation literature, informal classroom observations have been tied to both formative and summative evaluation practices. Manning (1988) asserted that information about teachers gleaned from "walking-around supervision" and "short visits" should be included as summative samplings in the overall evaluation of teaching. Although the two are similar, Manning makes a sharp distinction between walking-around supervision and short visits. Walking-around supervision promotes the visibility of the principal but primarily in the lunchrooms, "in the halls … before and after the first bell in the morning, and immediately before the dismissal bell in the afternoon" (p. 145). During these and other times, the principal takes in information about instruction and plans short visits if there is a need (e.g., a teacher who is having difficulties with classroom management or a teacher who is regarded as having an exemplary instructional method). According to Manning, short visits last longer, "less than a full class period." Also, "it is important to always follow up a short visit with a brief conference," especially "if a problem is noted, [so] the principal can discuss this … and plan for an additional evaluation" (p. 146).

Catch Teachers in the Act of Teaching

The principal does *not* conduct informal classroom visitations to catch the teacher off guard or to interrupt classroom activities. Informal classroom observations allow principals to affirm what teachers are doing right by encouraging them to keep up the momentum. Moreover, informal observations allow the principal and teacher to celebrate successes in teaching and student learning.

Informal observations are one way instructional supervisors can get to know their teachers. By observing teacher's work *in their classrooms*, principals can exert informed effort and energy to assist teachers beyond formally scheduled observations. Informal observations provide opportunities for supervisors to:

♦ motivate teachers;

♦ monitor instruction;

♦ be accessible and provide support; and

♦ keep informed about instruction in the school (Blasé & Blasé, 1998, pp. 108–109)

An Observation by Any Other Name

Sometimes referred to as *pop-ins, walk-ins,* or *drop-ins,* informal classroom observations have the following characteristics:

♦ They are brief, lasting approximately 15 to 20 minutes (perhaps longer).

♦ They can occur at the beginning, middle, or end of a period.

♦ They can occur at any time during the school day.

♦ They focus on a variety of aspects, including instruction, use of time, classroom management, transitions between learning activities, or the clarity of instructions.

Informal classroom observation is a strategy for getting into classrooms, with the intent of focusing on teaching, learning, and the interactions between teachers and students as the events of instruction unfold. As a strategy, the Center for Comprehensive School Reform and Improvement (2007) reports:

> The walk-through can be defined as a brief, structured non-evaluative classroom observation by the principal that is followed by a conversation between the principal and the teacher about what was observed. Used well, the walk-through can provide both principal and teacher with valuable information about the status of the school's instructional program. (p. 1)

A promising practice emerging in the field is the learning walk. The learning walk consists of teams of teachers, teacher leaders, and administrators who target grade levels or subject areas to conduct brief, 7- to 10-minute classroom observations as teams. The focus of the learning walk is to examine how teachers teach and how students learn. There is typically a focus for the learning walk—questioning strategies, wait time, variety of instructional strategies, classroom management, cooperative learning, differentiated instruction, and so on. The group conducts the learning walk, debriefs about the data for a few minutes and then as a group goes into another classroom for 7 to 10 minutes, debriefs, and the cycle continues. At the end of the day, the walk teams summarize the data and then engage in conversations with the teachers whose classrooms were observed.

Informal observations are not intended to supplant formal ones; they do not include a preobservation conference. Too often, however, informal classroom observations also forgo postobservation conferences. The value of the informal observation, which culminates with an opportunity to talk with teachers, is that principals can strengthen their relationships with teachers by communicating *something* about what was observed. In fact, a majority of informal observations should include some type of follow-up conversation about teaching and learning. Chapter 4 details tools that can be used to chronicle what is observed during informal classroom observations, and chapter 5 offers techniques for communicating what is observed, along with strategies to assist teachers in reflecting on their practices. Chapter 6 provides some insights on how principals can engage teachers in discussion about student work.

How Much Time Is Enough?

The interest in informal classroom observations was piqued by the Downey Informal Observation method in which principals spend 3 to 5 minutes observing a classroom (Downey, Steffy, English, Frase, & Poston, 2005). Although that method will certainly get supervision out of the main office, the principal is encouraged to spend more than 3 to 5 minutes in the classroom so that the principal and teacher have a meaningful experience. The brevity of the egg-timer approach to classroom observation minimizes data collection. It is preferable to conduct fewer but longer informal observations on a daily basis. This extra time will pay short- and long-term dividends—connecting with teachers while deriving a more accurate sense of the classroom activities observed. Another dividend is movement toward high-quality learning for the teachers who are entrusted to educate children.

The principal's daily struggle is to find time for mandatory formal classroom observations and informal classroom visits. Although no clear-cut solution to this problem applies across all school systems, many principals have found creative ways to make the most of their available human resources and to provide a supervisory program centered on teachers' needs. Cues to include the administrative team with informal classroom observations were discussed in chapter 1. A commitment to being more visible to teachers will be strengthened by the impact that classroom visitations can have on bolstering the instructional program.

LINK INFORMAL OBSERVATIONS TO SCHOOLWIDE INSTRUCTIONAL IMPROVEMENT EFFORTS

It is not uncommon for schools to identify an instructional focus and targeted strategies for the year. For principals who work with their teachers to identify instructional strategies to master for the year, informal classroom observations can be instrumental in helping the principal provide focused feedback to teachers. Because the principal gets out and about, she has the opportunity to see first-hand instructional efforts toward implementing strategies. During postobservation conferences, she has the opportunity to help teachers reflect on how these strategies are being implemented, provide the forum for joint exploration on refining instructional practices, to affirm the work teachers are doing help student learn.

At Creekland Middle School (Lawrenceville, GA, Gwinnett County Public Schools), principal Dr. Bill Kruskamp and the 170 teachers agreed that they would spend a year mastering six strategies, assess how these strategies were being implemented and refined, and then move forward with identifying more strategies to build on the original six:

- Collaboration;
- Differentiation;
- Student Engagement;
- Summarizing;
- Display of Student Work; and
- Essential Question (EQ).

With close to 3,000 students at Creekland Middle School, the largest middle school in the state of Georgia and one of the largest in the United States, the administrative team was aware that they had to make informal classroom observations purposeful and that they had to take every opportunity to connect the work of teachers to the overall schoolwide instructional improvement efforts.

To ensure that informal classroom observations focused on the six strategies, Bill Kruskamp and the six assistant principals developed their own informal classroom observation tool (see Tool 3).

Tool 3: Focused Informal Classroom Observations—
Creekland Middle School*

Teacher: *Lori Miller*

Date: *March 14, 2008*

Administrator: *Bill Kruskamp*

Class Period: 1 2 3 ④ 5 6 7 8

Common Classroom Expectations:

- ◆ Collaboration
- ◆ Differentiation
- ◆ Student Engagement
- ◆ Summarizing
- ◆ Display of Student Work
- ◆ Essential Question (EQ):

Expectation Domains	*Presence = X*
1. **Assessment:** Frequently assess students' learning of the AKS and gives specific feedback to the students and parents.	
2. **Nonverbal Representations:** Uses a variety of nonverbal/visual representations of content and skills.	
3. **Modeling and Practice:** Models strategies and skills. Provides multiple opportunities for distributed practice followed by independent practice.	*X*
4. **Vocabulary:** Explicitly teaches essential content-related vocabulary.	
5. **Summarizing:** Explicitly teaches students to summarize their learning.	*X*
6. **Collaboration:** Provides collaborative learning opportunities.	
7. **Student Goal Setting:** Teaches and requires students to set personal goals for improving their academic achievement.	
8. **Literacy:** Explicitly teaches skills for improving reading and writing proficiency/literacy across the content areas.	

Tool continues on next page.

Expectation Domains	Presence = X
9. **Problem-Solving:** Uses inquiry-based, problem-solving learning strategies with students in all content areas.	
10. **Questioning:** Uses and teaches questioning and cuing/ prompting techniques.	X
11. **Background Knowledge:** Accesses and/or builds students' background knowledge and experiences.	
12. **Comparison and Contrast:** Teaches students to compare and contrast knowledge, concepts, and content.	
13. **Technology:** Uses technology effectively to plan, teach, and assess.	

Comments:

Lori: Getting to higher-order questions supported your assessment in two ways: (1) students summarized what they had learned and (2) students were "stretched" to answer questions that showed mastery of content. For example, you asked, "What is democracy?", then you asked students to identify democratic practices in local politicians, and then you asked students: "How do you apply democratic principles in their everyday life?" I enjoyed the classroom observation. I will look for some materials that I may have regarding democracy that may help you."

Throughout the year, the administrative team debriefed to learn as a collective what was occurring instructionally at Creekland Middle School. From their discussions, professional development was geared to assist teachers master skills and then to focus, and in some instances refocus, their attention during subsequent informal classroom observations. Tool 4 illustrates a focus on the relationship between the essential question and summarizing.

---

*Used with permission. Dr. Bill Kruskamp, principal, Creekland Middle School, Gwinnett County Public Schools (Lawrenceville, GA).

Tool 4: Informal Classroom Observation: The Essential Question and Summarizing*—Creekland Middle School

Teacher: *Andy Bercher*

Date: *March 27, 2008*

Essential Questions: (Yes) No

- ◆ Posted
- ◆ Guides Instruction
- ◆ Used at the end of lessons to assist summarizing and gather evidence of learning.

Summarizing: (Yes) No

- ◆ Reflects evidence of student learning
- ◆ All students participating
- ◆ Guided by the essential questions

What the students were doing?

Students were working in pairs with manipulatives as they solved algebraic equations.

Comments:

Andy, you really had the students engaged in this lesson! When students reported out from their groups, it was clear that they were able to summarize their learning about balancing the two sides of the equation. I look forward to seeing where this lesson continues and students gain mastery.

Thanks—Bill

A treasure chest of classroom observation tools suitable for the informal classroom observation is offered later in this book.

---

*Used with permission. Dr. Bill Kruskamp, principal, Creekland Middle School, Gwinnett County Public Schools (Lawrenceville, GA).

GUIDELINES FOR INFORMAL CLASSROOM OBSERVATIONS

The following guidelines for informal classroom observations are offered as a starting point for framing this important work.

Guidelines for Informal Classroom Observations

Informally Observe All Teachers

All teachers can benefit from informal classroom observation. Refrain from "overobserving" particular teachers (e.g., only teachers who are having difficulty, beginning teachers, teachers who teach subject areas that are heavily tested). Informal classroom observation should last between 15 and 20 minutes; therefore, conduct only as many observations in a day as you can follow up on either the same day or the very next day. Teachers need and deserve some type of immediate feedback.

Informally Observe as Often as You Can

The principal's presence in classrooms sends a positive message to teachers: *the principal cares.* Including informal classroom observation as a schoolwide initiative requires consistency and frequency. Become opportunistic in finding time in the day to observe teachers, and vary the time of the day in which you observe teachers. What occurs in the morning is much different from what occurs in the afternoon.

Watch, Listen, and Write, but Focus on One or Two Areas

Although there is no predetermined focus established because there is no preobservation conference, find a focus based on the instruction, events, or discussions that are occurring in the classroom. As much as possible, avoid publicizing personal biases that may encourage teachers to "play to the audience." For example, if the principal is a proponent of cooperative learning, teachers might be tempted to transition to cooperative learning activities once the principal enters the room.

Given that informal observations are relatively brief (15–20 minutes) compared to an extended classroom observation (30–45 minutes), data from a single focus will make for richer conversation during follow-up discussion.

Guidelines for Informal Classroom Observations

Let it Be Obvious That You Are Having Fun

A principal's demeanor sends strong messages: either the principal enjoys being out and about, or the principal grudgingly engages in informal classroom observations. Let your body language and facial expressions communicate that you are enjoying the time in the classroom. Think about how you want teachers and students to view you.

Catch Them in the Act of Doing Something Right and Applaud Efforts

Look for victories rather than failures and applaud them. Work to create an ethos of sharing. Teachers who are especially adept at a strategy or technique need time and opportunities for sharing their expertise with others. For example, a certain amount of time at weekly or monthly faculty meetings could be set aside for teachers to share insights or techniques with one another.

Make the Time to Follow Up

Follow-up communication to informal classroom observation is a critical component. Through conversations and reflection, teachers better understand the complexities of their work. Feedback and dialogue form the cornerstone of all supervisory activities.

Follow Up With Resources

After feedback, the effective principal also makes available resources that teachers need to refine practice. The principal's efforts to return for a follow-up informal observation might be one such resource.

Make Informal Observations Invitational

Encourage teachers to invite you to observe them. Teachers who are experimenting with novel instructional approaches or whose students are making presentations would welcome the opportunity for the principal to be present.

Source: Adapted from FutureCents (2005).

Looking Ahead ...

The next chapter explores the intent of data collection and some broad techniques to consider before exploring and applying the classroom observation tools presented in chapter 4.

3
Understanding Data-Collection Techniques and Approaches

In This Chapter ...

+ Intent of data collection
+ Types of data and data-collection techniques

Fertile data can be gleaned from an informal classroom observation lasting between 15 and 20 minutes. More than merely watching during an informal observation, the principal collects stable and useful data. Accurate and bias-free data will further assist teachers in making sense of their teaching. The intent of data collection and data-collection techniques are examined in this chapter, and in chapter 4, the data-collection tools used during classroom observations will be applied.

INTENT OF DATA COLLECTION

The adage "less is more" is worth exploring given that an informal classroom observation lasts a relatively short time. Brevity, coupled with the fast-paced nature of activities in a classroom, dictates that the principal focus on less to provide a more detailed and richer portrayal of what occurred. Many types of data can be collected during an informal classroom observation. Consider the possibilities:

+ engagement of the learner through the content;
+ instructional methods used to deliver the content;
+ types of activities that engage learners;
+ resources used to enhance learning experiences; or
+ types of assessments used to make judgments about learning.

27

These areas and more are important to teaching and learning, and all deserve attention. According to McGreal (1988, pp. 21–22), there are four presuppositions of data collection that should drive the observation and the tools used to collect data.

1. The reliability and usefulness of classroom observation is related to the amount and types of information that supervisors have prior to the observation.

2. The narrower the focus that supervisors use in observing classrooms, the more likely they will be to describe the events related to that focus.

3. The impact of observational data is related to the way the data are recorded during the observation.

4. The impact of observational data on supervisor–teacher relationships is related to the way feedback is presented to the teacher.

The first presupposition applies more readily to a formal classroom observation that includes a preobservation conference in which the teacher and principal agree on a focus for the classroom observation. The predetermined focus drives the classroom observation and the techniques used to collect data.

During an informal classroom observation, the principal develops a focus on the spot, and this is why the principal is more than a mere observer. The principal becomes a silent but active participant, making a snap judgment about what to focus on and for how long. The broad focus of the classroom observation is dependent on what occurs in the classroom. Figure 3.1 examines some possibilities that the principal might focus on during an informal classroom observation.

Teaching is not an isolated enterprise; one area of instruction affects other areas (e.g., organizing for instruction affects student engagement). This is why the learning environment is exciting. Because teachers are engaged in the moments of teaching and make split-second decisions about what to do next based on student responses, they benefit from data, subsequent feedback, and opportunities to talk and reflect about teaching.

Types of Data

Data may be quantitative, qualitative, or a combination of both. Quantitative data includes frequencies, distributions, and other counts or tallies of information. Checklists are quantitative because they do not use words to describe what, how, or why something occurred. For example, the observer could use a checklist to tally how many questions were asked of children in the front row or how many times the teacher called on students whose hands were raised or not raised. Qualitative data could include scripted notes detailing patterns of activities, words, and other events observed. Whether data are quantitative or qualitative, accuracy is essential; the credibility of the process and the principal is at stake.

Figure 3.1. Focus Areas for Informal Classroom Observations

Broad Focus Area	Possible Target Points Within the Focus Area
Instructional methods and techniques	Cooperative learning, direct instruction, indirect instruction, questioning strategies, wait time
Organizing for instruction	Use of advance organizers, posing a problem, dilemma, or objective
Classroom procedures	Beginning and ending classroom procedures, transitions, physical proximity and movement
Student engagement and involvement	On- and off-task behavior, questioning strategies, use of student responses to extend discussion, maintaining student focus and attention
Subject matter and content	Organization, breadth, depth, and scope
Other	Use of technology and manipulatives

TYPES OF DATA AND DATA-COLLECTION TECHNIQUES

On entering the classroom, the principal makes two major decisions:

1. Where to focus attention during the observation; and
2. What observation technique(s) is best suited to collect and display this data?

These two considerations are interrelated because what the observer decides to focus on during the observation dictates which technique or tool is most suitable for collecting data. Regardless of the technique for data collection, always start small by focusing on one or two items, and take notes that relate directly to the items. Remember: Less is more!

Figure 3.2 provides an overview of the techniques used to collect data while observing teachers.

Wide-Angle and Narrow-Angle Methods

Acheson and Gall (1997) developed a series of data-collection tools that are classified as either wide-angle methods or narrow-angle methods, similar to the lenses available for use on a camera. In general, the *wide-angle methods* allow the principal to capture a larger picture, and the *narrow-angle methods* allow the principal to "zoom in" and collect more finite data focused on a one or two aspects. Figure 3.3 describes the six most commonly used data-collection tools developed by Acheson and Gall (1997).

Figure 3.2. Classroom Observation Data-Collection Techniques

Techniques	Description
Behavior category	A narrow set of behaviors is tracked
Checklist	A standardized form allows the principal to check which activities and behaviors are present or absent
Classroom diagramming	Classroom tracking of certain behaviors or movement of teachers and students are recorded in short increments of time
Selected verbatim notes	Words, questions, and interactions are recorded verbatim.
Open narrative	Anecdotal notes with or without a focus are recorded
Teacher-designed instrument	Teacher develops an instrument to audit certain teaching and learning behaviors.
Audiotape	The principal audiotapes the classroom, often taking notes or diagramming movement; the audio recording can be used to help reconstruct the events of the lesson
Videotape	The events of the classroom are videotaped and then viewed at a later time

Figure 3.3. Data-Collection Tools: An Overview of Methods

Type of Method/Lens	Data-Collection Tool	Focus
Narrow lens	Selective verbatim	Records words that were said by the teacher, the students, or both
Narrow lens	Verbal flow	Details the frequency of who spoke—how often and when
Narrow lens	At-task	Provides detail, noting periodically over time of who appears to be at-task
Narrow lens	Class traffic	Tracks the teachers' (or students') physical movement
Narrow lens	Interaction analysis	Provides detail about the types of statements made by either the teacher or the students
Wide lens	Anecdotal/global scan	Notes what was occurring overall in the classroom. This can become more subjective unless the supervisor records "just the facts"

Source: Adapted from Acheson and Gall (1997).

Narrow-Angle Methods and Tools

Narrow-angle data-collection methods have several tools, including selective verbatim, verbal flow, at-task, class traffic, and interaction analysis. These tools help the supervisor to collect data that detail which students are engaged by focusing on very specific types of data: words, frequency of words, student or teacher movement, and so forth. For example, if the principal enters a classroom in which the teacher engages students in a question-and-answer session, it is ideal to focus on what types of questions are asked. The principal narrows the observation technique to chronicle in detail the questions asked of students. Therefore, the principal needs to write, as verbatim as possible, the questions asked. The scope of data collected would typically be just the questions; however, the lens can widen to track not only the questions the teacher asks, but also the students' responses to the questions (see Figure 4.1, Bloom's Taxonomy).

Wide-Angle Methods and Tools

The most prevalent wide-angle tool is the *global scan,* which is useful for collecting information about the events of the class as they unfold. Data could include the words of the teacher and students, the physical activity of the teacher and students, the types of instructional methods used and their duration—or just about any other event or occurrence in the classroom. The global scan is intended to give the teacher a general sense of the classroom.

The strength of the wide-angle method of recording anecdotally is the ability to chronicle events as they occur. A weakness is the possibility that bias and value judgment may emerge as the events are being scripted. Consider the following two statements:

1. "While you were giving instructions for the small-group activity, one girl left her seat to sharpen a pencil."
2. "Your instructions were unclear so students tuned out. One girl began sharpening her pencil while you were talking, an effort to undercut your authority."

The first statement presents the facts without editorial speculation. The second statement is value laden; even its wording ("tuned out" and "undercut your authority") sends a negative message. How is the teacher likely to respond to each statement? Using the wide-angle method of scripting anecdotally requires a conscious effort to leave value judgments off the page.

And Data Are Important Because ...

Data collected during classroom observations tend to describe teacher and student behaviors using a series of snapshots, with each piece of data depicting isolated events that occurred during a teaching episode. It is the analysis of the data that permits the teacher and the supervisor to identify patterns through which a holistic image of teaching can be created. The key for success is to observe not only the teacher but also the students. Effective observation involves keeping one eye on the teacher and the other eye on the students, tracking the effect of teaching behaviors on student response and learning.

Show Me the Data!

Each data-collection tool has its strengths and limitations and yields different types of information about the events of the classroom observation. The following illustrates what data would look like using *select* data-collection tools described in Figure 3.3.

Selective verbatim focuses on specific words, questions, or responses of the teacher, students, or both. The first example focuses on the questions the teacher asks.

T: What were the events leading up to the crime?
T: Of these events, which event motivated the main character the most?
T: Why was this event the most important?
T: How would the ending of the book have been different if this event had not occurred?

The next example displays both the teacher's questions and the student's responses to the questions.

Teacher Questions	*Student Responses*
1. What were the events leading up to the crime?	1. The man was desperate, he had to feed his children; he lost his job; his oldest son was diagnosed with a life-threatening disease.
2. Of these events, which event motivated the main character the most?	2. The son's life-threatening disease.
3. Why was this event the most important?	3. He had no money to pay the doctor.

Another way the selective verbatim technique can be used is to categorize the teacher's responses as "praise," "correction," or "preventive prompts," followed by the time, as in the following example. The data in the following example (Tool 5) shed light not only on the teacher's statements but also on the patterns and routines for the beginning of the class period.

Tool 5:   Selective Verbatim:
Praise, Correction, and Preventive Prompts*

Teacher: **Bob Bennett**   Date of Observation: **February 25, 2008**

Observer: **Pat Montalvo**

Class: **Study and Life Skills**   Period of the Day: **Morning**

Time of Observation: Start: **9:40**   End: **9:50**

Total Time Spent in Observation: **10 minutes**

Number of Students Present: **11**   Grade level: **Sophomores**

Topic of the Lesson: **Teacher was readying the class to begin work**

Date of Postobservation Conference: **February 26, 2008**

Teacher Comment/Response	Time	Praise	Correction	Preventive Prompt
Please come in and get seated.	**9:40**			X
Bob, close the door and come in.	**9:41**		X	
Your pencils need to be sharpened before class.	**9:42**		X	
Looks like Jeff is ready to get started.	**9:43**	X		
Jack needs to stop talking and follow along.	**9:45**		X	
Louise is patiently waiting for us to begin.	**9:46**	X		
Guys, you need to get paper out and follow along.	**9:47**		X	
I see Martin is ready!	**9:48**	X		
I can't begin until every ones' attention is up here.	**9:49**		X	
Tony, take your hood off your head please.	**9:49**		X	

Tool continues on next page.

---

*Developed by Theresa L. Benfante, Behavior Interventionist at Central Alternative School, Cobb County School District (Georgia). Used with permission.

Teacher Comment/Response	Time	Praise	Correction	Preventive Prompt
We have wasted 10 minutes waiting for some of you to get ready.	9:50		X	
Leslie is ready to go.		X		
Bob and Jack, we are waiting for you to pay attention.			X	
Thanks Steve, I see you are ready.		X		
When you come to class prepared, we can begin on time.			X	X
Ratio of praise to correction: 5:9				
Preventive prompts: 2				

Global scan/anecdotal focuses on events, actions, or words of the teacher, students, or both. Data that are scripted can take many forms. To chronicle the events, only a blank sheet of paper, an eye, and ear are needed to capture the events of the class. Anecdotal notes can focus events as they unfold by time or just by events.

Anecdotal Data Sample—by Time

9:05	Teacher asked student (male, red shirt) to elaborate on the "yes" response.... How S. E. Hinton developed the symbol of the Siamese fighting fish.
9:06	Student: "at the end of the story... he sets the rumble fish free and then he dies ... the characters fight like the rumble fish."
9:07	Teacher asks a general question: "Are there are other examples through-out the book?" (several hands go up...teacher calls on student who is fidgeting with her backpack)

✓ Teacher was at the door when students entered the room.

✓ Students knew the routine: they went to their seats, pulled out books, note-books, and the homework assignment due (the agenda on the blackboard cued students on what to do to get ready for the period).

✓ When the bell rang, a student turned on the overhead projector; teacher pointed to the math problem—students began working on solving the word problem.

✓ Teacher took attendance, spoke briefly with a student at her desk, and walked up and down the aisles collecting homework assignments.

✓ Teacher focused students on the word problem—asked for the properties of the word problem before asking for the solution.

✓ Student in the back of the room (arm in cast) gave the answer to the word problem—320 pounds of coffee beans.

✓ Teacher asked student in front of the room to write the formula she used to get a different answer (285 was her response).

✓ As the student wrote the formula, teacher asked questions of another student who had the same answer.

✓ Student at the board "talked through" her answer and the steps she took to derive the answer.

✓ The teacher enlisted other students for answers to questions.

✓ Teacher transitioned the class to a page in their books—modeled how to analyze the word problem—wrote numbers on the board, enlisted students with helping her with the computations.

The next open-ended data collection tool is another way to landscape classroom observation notes.

Tool 6:   Open-Ended Classroom Observation Form*

Lakesha Williams	January 16, 2008	9:05–9:15
Teacher's Name	Date	Beginning and Ending Times
Band—Period 2	7	Band Room
Subject / Period	Grades	Location
General		Sr. Florence
Objectives to be observed. If none specified, write, "general."		Observer's Name

Times	Observations
9:05	Students moved quickly and efficiently once they had their instruments.
9:08	Warm-up. Students performed warm-up exercises together.
9:10	Sally was asked where her instrument (clarinet) was. Response: "I left it at home." Teacher reminded Sally that this was the third time this month. Sally became upset and was sent to the counselor.
9:15	Teacher returned to the lesson with the large group.

Times	Observations (continued)
	Additional Observations

The next classroom observation form (Tool 7) is open-ended but includes key areas such as learning objective, instructional strategies, seating arrangement, and so forth, to focus the observation. Obviously, in a 15 to 20 minute classroom observation, a principal would not be able to comment on all of these areas; however, the areas are important ones to focus attention during an informal classroom observation.

Tool 7: Open-Ended—Key Areas

Teacher: **Jose Hernandez**   Date of Observation: **January 31, 2008**

Observer: **Gregory Torchenski**

Class: **Health**   Period of the Day: **4th**

Time of Observation: Start: **11:30**   End: **11:40**

Total Time Spent in Observation: **10 minutes**

Number of Students Present: **24**   Grade level: **9th (girls)**

Topic of the Lesson: **Weight Management/Nutrition**

Date of Postobservation Conference: **February 1, 2008**

I. Learning Objective: **Appropriate eating and physical activities that support weight management (posted on white board and handout).**

II. Instructional Strategies (also note time):   **11:30–11:37 lecture on calories and physical activity to burn calories. Had students stand and run in place for 1 minute. Led discussion on the amount of physical activity needed to maintain or lose weight.**

III. Seating Arrangement:

IV. Transition Strategies: **Cued students "stand and run briskly" and blew whistle to stop running in place.**

V. Calling Patterns:

VI. Markers of Student Engagement: **All students were engaged. The physical activity was a positive way to illustrate calorie burning.**

Checklists

A narrow data-collection method is the *checklist* approach, in which data are usually tallied at the end so that patterns can be inferred; however, checklist data also can be descriptive. A sample of checklist data is detailed in Tool 8.

Tool 8: Sample Checklist Classroom Observation Form

Teacher: **Nancy Chandley**   Date of Observation: **February 12, 2008**

Observer: **Martine Orozco**

Class: **English 1**   Period of the Day: **Block 2**

Time of Observation: Start: **10:25** End: **10:45**

Total Time Spent in Observation: **20 minutes**

Number of Students Present: **26**   Grade Level: **Freshman**

Topic of the Lesson: **Writing narrative essays**

Date of Postobservation Conference: **February 13, 2008**

Students were
- ☐ working in small, cooperative groups
- ☐ making a presentation
- ☐ taking a test
- ☒ working independently at their desks
- ☐ viewing a film
- ☐ other _____

Teacher was
- ☐ lecturing
- ☐ facilitating a question and answer sequence
- ☒ working independently with students
- ☐ demonstrating a concept
- ☐ introducing a new concept
- ☐ reviewing for a test
- ☐ coming to closure
- ☐ other _____

Comments: *Nancy:*

- ♦ *Students were working independently at their desks.*

- ♦ *The arrangement of the room (desk, podium, table) allowed you to work independently with students on their essays and to keep an eye on students working at their desks.*

    Perhaps you should hold the next freshman-level meeting in your room so others can see your room arrangement.

    Thanks for letting me visit your room and see the work you do to help our students become better writers. I appreciate your efforts.

    —*Martine Orozco*

Tool 9 provides another example of a mixed-method informal classroom observation instrument.

Tool 9:   Mixed-Method Informal Classroom Observations—
Daves Creek Elementary School
Informal Teacher Observation Form*

Teacher's Name: **Stephanie Baker**   Date of Observation: **March 17, 2008**
Administrator: **Roger Clarke**   Time: **8:01 to 8:12**

Learning Environment:

Presence/ Absence	Criteria	Example Evidence
X	1. Neat/well organized; safety information posted; Gotta Go Bag accessible	**Room was set up so students could move to different areas without incident.**
	2. Artifacts—standards/curriculum-based, level appropriate, incorporate student work	
	3. Essential questions relating to lesson posted in an area for students to see	
X	4. Classroom rules clearly posted with rewards/consequences	**Posted prominently on white board.**
	5. Transitions are appropriate and smooth	
X	6. Routines and procedures are in place and followed	**Students knew how and where to put books and coats before going to seats.**
	7. Students show engagement to current lesson or task	
	8. Mutual respect is evident	

Tool continues on next page.

---

*This tool was developed by Eric Ashton, principal, and Peggy Baggett, assistant principal of Daves Creek Elementary School, and Kathy Carpenter now principal at Riverwatch Middle School in Forsyth County Public Schools (GA). Used with permission.

Lesson Design and Delivery Incorporates the
WOW* Design Qualities and Differentiation

Presence/ Absence	Criteria	Example Evidence
	9. Varied strategies and use of graphic organizers are used to meet needs of diverse learners— ESOL, EIP, special ed, and gifted	
✗	10. Student work is meaningful and has "real-life" application	*Great anticipatory comments on the lesson "caring for others" by using pet analogies.*
	11. Students are provided with specific and descriptive feedback throughout lesson to target areas of improvement	
✗	12. Varied levels of student work samples are posted for the purpose of student self-assessing against standards	*Separate bulletin board for displaying student work.*
✗	13. Support for reading and math AIM goals is evident	*There are many posters for reflecting goals.*
	14. Guided Reading Lessons: Small group reading purpose before and after Running reading records Genre Graphic organizers Questions/critical thinking	
	15. Variety of student grouping used to meet individual student needs	

Comments:

Stephanie, It was good to see how students respond to your expectations for the day, especially since this is the first day back from spring break.

The following checklist (Tool 10) was developed for supervisors and literacy coaches during informal and formal classroom observations.

---

*WOW is "Working on the Work," a reform construct developed by Phil Schlechty (see *Shaking Up the Schoolhouse*, 2000).

Tool 10: Literacy Classroom Observation Checklist*

Teacher: **Emily Watkins**   Date of Observation: **January 24, 2008**   Observer: **Pat Dooley**

Time of Observation: Start: **10:15**   End: **10:30**   Total Time Spent in Observation: **15 minutes**

Number of Students Present: **18**   Grade Level: **4th Grade**   Topic of the Lesson: **Word Recognition**

Date of Postobservation Conference: **January 25, 2008**

Literacy Block	Guided Reading	Well Organized Classroom	Literacy Rich Classroom
___ Read Aloud	___ Small Group area evident	**X** Posts & uses rules, schedules, management system	___ Print-rich environment
___ Phonemic Awareness (K-2)	___ Uses appropriate narrative texts	___ Students routinely follow established rules & procedures	___ Concept charts
___ Concepts of Print (K-2)	___ Uses appropriate informational texts	**X** Smooth transitions	**X** Definition charts
___ Shared Reading	___ Differentiates instruction to meet all students' needs	___ Room organized, labeled	___ 6+1 Traits posters
___ Guided Reading	___ Uses before, during, after activities	___ Seating arranged for cooperative learning activities and interaction	**X** Comprehension posters
___ Centers/Independent Work	___ Incorporates comprehension	**X** Students accountable for learning	___ Authentic reading/writing observed
___ Monitored Independent Reading (MIR)	___ Incorporates fluency	**X** Room clutter free, inviting	___ Student writing displayed
X Explicit whole-class instruction	___ Teaches vocabulary of text	**X** Productive, workable noise level	___ Classroom library evident, with narrative & informational texts in a wide variety of genres, leveled appropriately, for student use
X Word Work	___ Listens to students read	**X** Teacher has positive interaction with students	___ Leveled book boxes for MIR
X Phonics/Spelling	___ Conducts running records	**X** Positive interaction between students	**X** Word Wall posted, consisting of general and content words
X Comprehension	___ Has up-to-date records		
___ Fluency	___ Uses appropriate reading strategies (whisper, staggered, choral, paired, etc.) NO ROUND-ROBIN reading!		
___ Oral Language			
___ Interactive/Shared Writing			
___ Modeled Writing			
___ Directed Writing			
___ 6+1 Traits of Writing			
___ Writer's Workshop			
___ Independent Writing			

Centers/Independent Work
- Management system in place
- Students responsible for learning
- Engaging activities
- Authentic reading/writing activities
- Student accountability system
- Differentiated work matches student needs
- Work reinforces previously taught concepts

Explicit Instruction
- X Grade-Level teacher talk
- Shared Reading- all students
- Uses Houghton Mifflin for shared reading
- Other grade-level texts (Big Books, poetry, informational)
- X All students have access to text
- Book Talk
- Preteaches vocabulary
- X Use comprehension strategies before, during, after activities
- Interactive, hands-on activities
- Integrated content core
- Incorporates good ESL strategies

Writing
- Writing Process
- Mini Lesson
- 6+1 Traits of Writing
- Student Accountability/status of class
- Interactive/shared writing (K-2)
- Modeled Writing
- Directed Writing
- Independent Writing
- Student published writing available to other students
- Writing area & materials evident

MIR
- Minimum 15-20 minutes per day
- Students self-select books from independent reading level-interest based books provided by teacher
- Variety of genres provided
- Monitoring, nongraded (student reflections, cooperative learning discussions, conferences, bookmarks, journals, pictures, etc.)

Word Work
- Phonemic Awareness (K-2)
- Phonics
- X Vocabulary
- X Differentiated Spelling
- Grade-level Language Arts
- X Word Wall posted
- X Word Wall systematically used in instruction

Assessment
- X Keeps up-to-date running records with guided reading levels
- Submits guided reading levels as requested
- X Maintains detailed formal and informal assessment records
- Maintains list of below level students

Collaboration
- Collaborates with team in analyzing assessment data
- Collaboratively plans for/provides interventions, reteaching, enrichment, differentiation

Curriculum Mapping
- Creates curriculum map, based on Utah State Core and student needs
- Uses curriculum map to guide instruction

*This tool was developed by the Jordan School District, Sandy, UT. Acknowledgement is given to Dana L. Bickmore, executive director for curriculum and staff development and Kathy Ridd, elementary language arts and early childhood consultant of the Jordan School District. Used with permission.

The strength of the checklist method is its ease of use; the principal takes in information and checks off what was observed or heard during the observation period. A weakness is that it is often difficult to reduce words or actions to a predetermined category on a checklist form. Moreover, checklist data—although easy to tally or look for patterns of occurrence of events (e.g., how many times students raised their hands, the number of questions asked)—can limit room for describing or giving specific detail about the events observed. The checklist has its place and enables the principal to be more efficient when making observations.

Mixed-Method Data-Collection Techniques

Combining scripted (anecdotal) and checklist methods provide both qualitative and quantitative data about what was observed. Tool 11 offers a sample of how both open-ended (scripted) and narrow (checklist) data can be combined to chronicle the events of the classroom.

Tool 11: Anecdotal and Checklist Data-Collection Method, Focus on Cooperative Learning

Teacher: **Janie Adams**   Date of Observation: **April 25, 2008**
Observer: **Antonio Tanuta**
Time of Observation: Start: **9:05**   End: **9:25**
Total Time Spent in Observation: **20 minutes**
Number of Students Present: **26**   Grade Level: **Juniors**
Topic of the Lesson: **Examining how a bill is passed**
Date of Postobservation Conference: **April 28, 2008**

Focus	Presence = X Absence = 0	Notes
Objectives for the cooperative learning group	X	✓ Objective for the activity was written on the white-board. ✓ Teacher referred to the objective as students asked questions. ✓ Teacher returned to the objective during closure of group activity.
Clarity of directions	X	✓ Before breaking students into groups, teacher gave directions. ✓ Teacher distributed directions for each group once students moved into their groups.
Movement into groups	X	✓ Six minutes for students to move into groups. ✓ Materials were bundled for each group in advance.
Monitoring and intervening strategies	X	✓ Teacher turned lights on and off to get attention. ✓ Teacher broke into group time three times with clarifying directions. ✓ Teacher visited each group four times.
Interaction with students	X	✓ Asked questions and gave feedback to groups while monitoring. ✓ Became a member of each group.
Follow-up instruction	X	✓ After 19 minutes, teacher called end to group work. ✓ Students moved desks and chairs back in order.

Tool 12 presents an open-ended form for collecting data in a foreign language classroom.

Tool 12:   Foreign Language Observation Checklist*

Teacher: *Marianna Smith*   Date of Observation: *April 10, 2008*
Observer: *Johann Frederickson*
Class: *French 2*   Period of the Day: *4*
Time of Observation: Start: *12:30*   End: *12:50*
Total Time Spent in Observation: *20 minutes*
Number of Students Present: *28*   Grade Level: *9 & 10*
Topic of the Lesson: *French teenagers*
Date of Postobservation Conference: *April 11, 2008*

1. Are all language modalities evident in the lesson (speaking, writing, listening, and reading)?

   ♦ *Students heard a passage read by the teacher, then spoke with a partner or in a group of three to collectively summarize (in writing) the gist of the reading.*

2. Is culture evident in the lesson?

   ♦ *Because the passage was about French teens, culture was evident.*

3. Does the teacher use a wide variety of prepared and authentic materials at appropriate levels?

   ♦ *The reading was taken from an authentic French source—a Parisian teen magazine.*

   ♦ *Students were able to recreate the gist, so the level was apparently suitable for these learners.*

4. Is the purpose of each activity clearly explained to the students?

   ♦ *The activity had already begun when I entered. However, students seemed to have a clear understanding of what they were doing.*

5. Does the teacher model activities when giving directions and check for comprehension afterward?

   ♦ *Marianna gave directions before and after each of the two times she read the passage.*

   ♦ *When students had finished rewriting the passage summaries, three groups shared their summaries aloud with the class, and class mem-*

---

*Developed by Marcia Wilbur, PhD, executive director, Curriculum and Content Development for the Advanced Placement Program at the College Board, based on her work at Gull Lake High School Foreign Language Department, Richland, Michigan. Used with permission.

bers commented on the accuracy of information, making suggestions to augment, improve, and/or clarify the content of each.

♦ *Marianna validated the information given, praised the students for their good work, and made suggestions for improvement.*

6. Are the transitions between activities smooth?

♦ *I only observed the passage summary activity.*

♦ *The class was preparing to move to a new activity when I left the room.*

♦ *The steps in the summary activity went smoothly from one to the next.*

7. Are the students on task and actively involved in the learning process?

♦ *Most students worked cooperatively with their partners.*

♦ *I noticed that there were three groups of three. In two of those groups, one student appeared to be much less involved than the other two students in the grouping.*

♦ *Because only one student was writing per group, I suggest breaking up the groups of three and sticking to pairs for this particular activity so that as many students as possible are highly engaged in the process.*

8. Is there an appropriate use of partner–pair or small group activities?

♦ *Yes, students worked in pairs (or groups of three as described above) with some brief moments of teacher-centered talk for the reading, directions, and feedback.*

The Seating Chart

An efficient way to collect data is to use the seating chart. Generic seating charts can be made in advance, or teachers can be asked to provide a general seating chart of their rooms at the beginning of the year. Several techniques for observing student and teacher behaviors make good use of the seating chart to collect data. Advantages for using the seating chart to chronicle data include the following:

♦ Ease of use: A seating chart can be drawn within half a minute of entering the room. Amount of data: A large amount of information can be recorded on a single chart. (Consider breaking up the observation into 5-minute increments—it is easy to get 5 minutes' worth of data on a single seating chart).

♦ Focus on the events: Important aspects of student behavior can be recorded while observing the teacher and the class as a whole.

If using the seating chart, it makes sense to have 15 to 20 copies available. The following generic seating chart (Tool 13) will assist you in collecting data. The observer can quickly sketch a seating chart upon entering the classroom.

Tool 13: Sample Seating Chart

Teacher: *Marianna Smith*   Date of Observation: *April 10, 2008*

Observer: *Johann Frederickson*

Class: *French 2*   Period of the Day: *4*

Time of Observation: Start: *12:30*   End: *12:50*

Total Time Spent in Observation: *20 minutes*

Number of Students Present: *28*   Grade Level: *9 & 10*

Topic of the Lesson: *French teenagers*

Date of Postobservation Conference: *April 11, 2008*

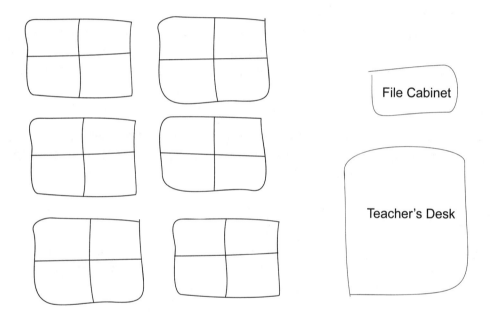

Some examples of data that can be recorded easily on a seating chart include:

♦ student–teacher question patterns;
♦ reinforcement and feedback; or
♦ classroom movement patterns.

Using the seating chart to track question patterns can provide data on whether the teacher focuses only on a few students on one side of the room. The seating chart also can be used to track classroom movement patterns to determine whether the teacher lectures from the front of the room only, or the types and frequency of feedback and reinforcement given to students.

Use Technology to Assist With Tracking Classroom Observation Data

Advances in technology can enhance the collection of data during classroom observations. Observers can enter data on a handheld device, import the data to a laptop, and print the data collected during a classroom observation. Follow-up notes can be communicated prior to the postobservation conference using e-mail.

With the prevalence of the laptop computer with built-in and external recording device capabilities, principals can use the laptop not only to take notes during observations but also to videotape teaching. When tools are combined with the features offered by computer database and spreadsheet applications, a rich rendition of teaching can be captured. The Synchronous Clinical Observation Music Tool* offers the opportunity to capture the series of events that involve teachers and students. These events or "sets of communication" (Gagné, Briggs, & Wager, 1992) occur on the canvas of time. Principals can make observations much more valuable when the observations are connected to accurate references of time. Computer time clocks have the capability to automate the collection of time data, thereby improving observation precision and usability of data for review in the postobservation conference. The Synchronous Clinical Observation Music Tool is a database application that uses Filemaker Pro and Quicktime Pro. This tool connects anecdotal, numerical, and video data to the internal clock of a laptop computer. Video is collected from an attached Web camera that records into Quicktime Pro. Filemaker Pro generates timestamps for each observation entry (referred to as a record). Automating timing and video functions allows the supervisor to focus on those aspects of the classroom that are under investigation.

Anecdotal observation is a versatile technique that is made more powerful when it is connected with time coding and video. The Synchronous Clinical Observation Music Tool allows the supervisor to enter text about events of the classroom to be analyzed during the postobservation conference (Tool 14 on the next page).

---

*The Synchronous Clinical Observation Music Tool was developed by Kevin Shorner-Johnson, a doctoral candidate in the Music Education Department at the University of Georgia. Used with permission.

Tool 14: Synchronous Clinical Observation Music Tool

Revisiting the video allows the teacher and supervisor to replay specific events when more contextual data are desired (Figure 3.4 on next page). The Synchronous Clinical Observation Music Tool can be used to analyze the rate/speed of teacher speech, question wait time, teacher movement, and activity pacing, as well as compare time spent in different types of teacher and student activities.

When numerical classroom data are paired with time codes, the frequencies of classroom events can be analyzed and later graphed using Microsoft Excel. Teachers frequently request an observation focus related to classroom management practices. Synchronous observation tools can collect data on the number of off-task students at any point in a timed manner. If measurements of off-task behavior are made frequently (at a recommended rate of 1 observation per 20 seconds), the principal can generate a descriptive report of off-task behaviors.

Figure 3.4. Analysis of Calculated Percent of Students On-Task

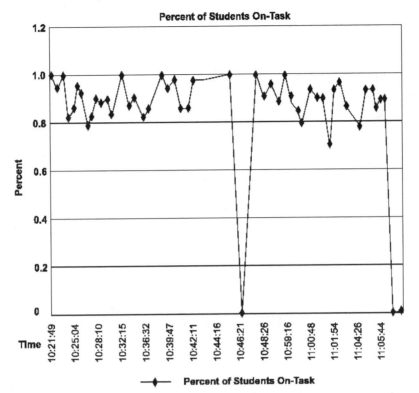

As example, a principal and a first-year choral teacher could use the synchronous off-task tool to identify problems and strengths in classroom management. Using a laptop computer, the principal records activity descriptions, counts of off-task students, and lets the computer provide time-stamp codes.

The principal could present the collected data using a table, line chart as illustrated in Figure 3.4. Data could also be presented using a histogram (Figure 3.5 on next page).

The principal would be able to present an overview of the timings, descriptions, numbers of off-task students, and percentage of on-task students. The line chart could identify trends of off-task behavior over time. To identify the relationship between off-task behaviors and groups of time (classroom activities), the principal could calculate averages of off-task behavior for each activity. A histogram could then be constructed using Microsoft Excel to illustrate differences in student activities.

During the postobservation conference, the teacher and principal could use the histogram chart (Figure 3.5) to generate discussion about student off-task behavior. The teacher would be able to identify that students were most on-task when they were singing in the classroom, and least engaged when the teacher was modeling a vocal technique.

Future advances in technology will help principals capture the events of the classroom more reliably. However, there are a few caveats to consider when using

Figure 3.5. Portrayal of Computer-Generated Data Using a Histogram

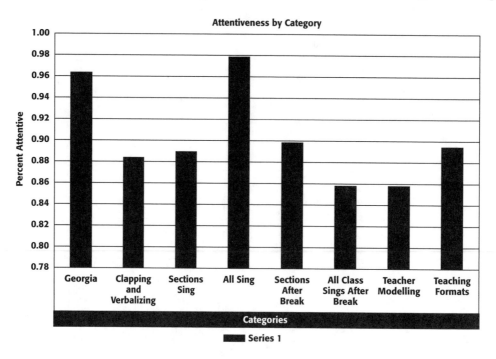

technology to capture the events of the classroom. First, the availability of technology might be limited, and the principal might need to find funding sources to purchase a laptop, video camera, and other software applications. Second, at first, teachers might not want to be videotaped, so it is best to ask before taping. There also might be union considerations to consider. In some systems, classroom observers can only observe without taking notes. Third, some systems strictly forbid students from being videotaped without written permission of parents. Fifth, principals would need to be trained in the uses of technology and have the opportunity to practice the skills needed to use technology to support classroom observations.

Whichever method of data collection is chosen, it is a good idea to detail major events such as teacher questions and student responses. A few strong examples with complete and accurate information will make more sense for both the teacher and the principal than will a long record of unfiltered information.

Looking Ahead ...

The next chapter explores data-collection tools that the principal can use while stepping out to observe teachers.

4
Looking in
While Stepping Out

In This Chapter ...

♦ Data collection tools and their applications

Teachers want the facts; they need to be able to examine and reflect on what these data mean during follow-up conversations with the principal (see chapter 5). Understanding and applying the tools of data collection, the principal has firm footing to conduct informal observations that can help teachers focus on their classroom practices.

DATA-COLLECTION TOOLS AND THEIR APPLICATION

Several tools are available and detailed here that will help principals track data from informal classroom observations. Unless otherwise indicated, the tools in this section are modified from the first edition of this book and from the second editions of *The Principal as Instructional Leader: A Handbook for Supervisors* (Zepeda, 2007a) and *Instructional Supervision: Applying Tools and Concepts* (Zepeda, 2007b). To illustrate these applications, each description includes the following:

♦ background;
♦ observation focus;
♦ observation technique;
♦ explanation of the tool and technique;
♦ how and why the technique is helpful;
♦ directions and approaches for using the tool;
♦ where appropriate, alternative data-collection techniques and tools to extend data collection;

- tips for using the technique; and
- suggested postobservation conference strategies.

The following data-collection tools can help you track data from classroom observations. Principals are encouraged to use their imaginations and revise these forms to develop unique renditions appropriate to the particular classroom contexts in their school: subject areas, grade levels, and the personnel teaching (e.g., teacher and paraprofessional, regular and special education coteaching partners). As a reminder, there are two decisions that are made when entering a classroom during an informal classroom observation:

1. Where to focus the observation based on what is occurring in the classroom; and

2. What data-collection tool or strategy to use to capture a rich portrayal of the events of the classroom.

Given that this book is promoting informal classroom observations, the principal who is out and about will be likely to conduct several informal classroom observations a day; therefore, tracking critical information about each observation is important. For each informal classroom observation, the following information should be noted in addition to the data collected during the observation:

- teacher name;
- observer name;
- date of the observation;
- period of the day;
- title of class;
- grade level;
- beginning time of the observation;
- ending time of the observation;
- total time spent in observation;
- number of students present;
- topic of the lesson; and
- date of postobservation conference.

This information is helpful when following up with the teacher and tracking which teachers are being observed and when. As a time-management strategy, this information helps the principal to determine the time of the day observations are occurring. For example, at the end of a month, the principal is able to determine whether more informal classroom observations were conducted in the morning or the afternoon or whether the observations were evenly distributed throughout the day. Moreover, such a tracking system ensures that all teachers benefit from informal classroom observations.

OBSERVATION GUIDE USING BLOOM'S TAXONOMY— CALL AND RESPONSE BACKGROUND

Teachers spend much time talking with students—lecturing, giving directions, and asking and answering questions. To ensure understanding and application of knowledge, teachers commonly engage students in question-and-answer sessions (also referred to as call and response or Q&A). Questions can prompt responses ranging from simple recall of information to abstract processes of applying, synthesizing, and evaluating information. Bloom (1956) and his colleagues developed a continuum for categorizing questions and responses. Bloom's taxonomy includes the following elements, arranged from lowest to highest order:

♦ *Knowledge:* recalling specific facts;

♦ *Comprehension:* describing in one's own words;

♦ *Application:* applying information to produce some result;

♦ *Analysis:* subdividing something to show how it is put together;

♦ *Synthesis:* creating a unique, original product; and

♦ *Evaluation:* making value decisions about issues.

Bloom's Taxonomy frames the analysis of both written and oral questions. Figure 4.1, provides an overview of Bloom's Taxonomy of questioning. Note that the continuum represents lower-order to higher-order thinking. Asking the right question is more important than getting the right answer. By focusing on questioning and answering segments during a lesson, the classroom observer will be able to help the teacher analyze not only the questions but also the types of responses. By reviewing classroom observation notes, the teacher can examine student responses (e.g., higher order questions with higher order responses or the converse, lower order questions with lower order responses). Moreover, the teacher will be able to assess student understanding and mastery and areas that might need to be retaught.

Framing questions that are challenging, open-ended, and uncluttered with extraneous information supports higher order thinking (Wang & Ong, 2003), and this is why examining both the teacher's questions and student responses to these questions is important. Three classroom observation tools (Tool 15, Tool 16, and Tool 18) are offered to assist the classroom observer track questions and student responses.

Figure 4.1. Bloom's Taxonomy

Bloom's Taxonomy and Definition	Sample Verb Stems	Students' Responses Would Indicate Skills Such As
Lowest Order		
Knowledge/Recall: Students are asked to remember information.	Summarize, describe, interpret	Memorizing, recognizing, identifying, and recalling
Comprehension: Students demonstrate they have understanding to organize and arrange material.	Classify, discuss, explain, identify, indicate, locate, report, restate, review, translate	Interpreting; translating from one medium to another; describing in one's own words; organizing and selecting facts and ideas
Application: Students apply previously learned information to reach an answer to a different but similar problem.	Apply, choose, demonstrate, dramatize, employ, illustrate, interpret, operate, practice, schedule, sketch, solve	Solving problems; applying information to produce an end product
Analysis: Students critically examine events and perform certain operations such as separating whole to part or part to whole.	Analyze, calculate, categorize, compare, contrast, criticize, differentiate, discriminate, examine, question	Subdividing, finding, identifying, and separating a whole into parts
Synthesis: Students produce an original work, make predictions, and/or solve problems.	Arrange, create, assemble, design, compose, develop, construct, formulate, manage, organize, plan, prepare, propose	Creating an original production
Highest Order		
Evaluation: Students answer a question that does not have an absolute answer, provide an educated guess about the solution to a problem, or render a judgment or opinion with backup support.	Appraise, argue, assess, attach, defend, judge, rate, support, value, evaluate	Making a decision, prioritizing information, drawing a conclusion

OBSERVATION GUIDE USING BLOOM'S TAXONOMY

Observation focus: Questioning strategies based on the class discussion

Observation technique: Selective verbatim

Explanation of the tool and technique: Selective verbatim is a narrow-lens tool that allows the observer to focus on select words of the teacher, the student, or both.

How and why the technique is helpful: This technique is helpful to give teachers feedback about the types of questions and the frequency of the types of questions asked. This technique can also assist the teacher in examining the levels of understanding and comprehension of content based on student responses. This technique can also shed light on the proportion of higher and lower order questions asked over a specified time.

Directions and approaches for using the tool: Using Tool 15, the principal records only the questions the teacher asks of students. Write the sentence in the left-hand column. Put a check in the box that best describes the cognitive level of the question. (This may be part of the postobservation conference.)

Tool 15: Observation Guide Using Bloom's Taxonomy

Teacher: **Anita Rodriguez**　　　　Date of Observation: **April 2, 2008**

Observer: **Frank Taylor**

Class: **Mathematics**　　　　Period of the Day: **Morning Block**

Time of Observation:　Start: **10:10**　　End: **10:30**

Total Time Spent in Observation: **20 minutes**

Number of Students Present: **17**　　Grade Level: **4th grade**

Topic of the Lesson: **Decimals**

Date of Postobservation Conference: **April 3, 2008**

		Levels of Thinking					
Time	Questions and Activities	KNOWLEDGE	COMPREHENSION	APPLICATION	ANALYSIS	SYNTHESIS	EVALUATION
10:10	How many have heard the word decimal?	✓					
	What do you think decimals mean?	✓					
	How do you know?		✓				
	Have you ever seen a decimal?	✓					
	What do you think that means?	✓					
	Why the decimal? Why that period?		✓				

Tool continues on next page.

Time	Questions and Activities	K N O W L E D G E	C O M P R E H E N S I O N	A P P L I C A T I O N	A N A L Y S I S	S Y N T H E S I S	E V A L U A T I O N
						Levels of Thinking	
	Decimal points do what?	✓					
10:15	What makes the cents, not the dollar?	✓					
	Why is 99 cents not a dollar?		✓				
	How would you write $200?	✓					
	What does "00" mean?	✓					
10:25	Is that where Desmond saw a decimal point?	✓					
	What instrument … temperature?	✓					
	How many kinds of therm? Name 2.	✓					
	What is she looking for?	✓					
	What is a normal temperature?	✓					
10:30	Have you seen your temperature written?	✓					
	Why do you think you need to use a decimal point?		✓				

Suggested Postobservation Conference Strategies

To promote engagement in the postobservation conference, Mr. Taylor brought the form to the conference with only the verbatim questions listed. Mr. Taylor encouraged Ms. Rodriguez to

♦ Identify the level of thinking for each question noted and then to place a check mark in the grid (e.g., knowledge, comprehension, application, synthesis, evaluation);

♦ Tally the number of questions at each level; and

♦ Rework a few of the lower-order questions into higher-order questions.

Throughout the last step, Mr. Taylor asked probing questions: "What did you eventually want students to be able to do with the information being taught?" "How did the examples presented along with the questions help students understand the materials?" "Are there any clusters of questions that could have been extended beyond the knowledge level?"

Mr. Taylor relied on the data to lead the discussion. He let Ms. Rodriguez analyze the data, reflect on what the data meant for student learning, and rework questions that she had asked. Viewed within the framework of Bloom's Taxonomy, these questions enabled Ms. Rodriguez to reconstruct her instruction in terms of her focus—levels of questions.

During the last 20 minutes of the postobservation conference, Mr. Taylor and Ms. Rodriguez targeted a few strategies to try before the next classroom observation. Of the ideas discussed, Ms. Rodriguez chose the following two:

1. Have a colleague videotape a lesson that includes a question-and-answer segment. Watching the video, record the questions she asked. Analyze the cognitive level of student responses and identify any patterns in what she asked of her students.

2. Use a professional release day to observe a teaching colleague at another school in the district.

Tips

♦ During the observation, write the question, and then in the postobservation conference, have the teacher identify the level of thinking for each question noted.

♦ An alternative strategy is to ask the teacher to rework a lower-order question into a higher-level question. Go back and forth.

Another way to landscape data using a more wide-angle lens related to teacher questions and the level of questions is presented in Tool 16. During the postobservation conference, ask the teacher to identify the taxonomy level.

Tool 16: Alternative Observation Guide Using Bloom's Taxonomy

Teacher: **Anita Rodriguez**   Date of Observation: **April 2, 2008**

Observer: **Frank Taylor**

Class: **4th grade**   Period of the Day: **Morning Block**

Time of Observation: Start: **10:10**   End: **10:30**

Total Time Spent in Observation: **20 minutes**

Number of Students Present: **17**   Grade Level: **4th grade**

Topic of the Lesson: **Decimals**

Date of Postobservation Conference: **April 3, 2008**

Time	Teacher Questions	Taxonomy Level
8:10	How many have heard the word "decimal"?	
	What do you think decimals mean?	
	How do you know?	
	Have you ever seen a decimal?	
	What do you think that means?	
	Why the decimal? Why that period?	
10:15	Decimal points do what?	
	What makes the cents, not the dollar?	
	Why is 99 cents not a dollar?	
10:25	How would you write $200?	
	What does "00" mean?	
	Is that where Desmond saw a decimal point?	
	What instrument ... temperature?	
	How many kinds of therm? Name 2.	
10:30	What is she looking for?	
	What is a normal temperature?	
	Have you seen your temperature written?	
	Why do you think you need to use a decimal point?	

FOCUS ON WAIT TIME

Background

A staple in teaching is the lecture and discussion, in which student response carries the rate and pace of the experience. Teachers, noticing cues from students, make adjustments in the pace and pitch of the classroom discussion. At the heart of lecture, discussion, and group processing of knowledge is the asking of questions. How the teacher responds to questions is important for two reasons: The quality of response is related to wait time, and the quality of the answer is related to wait time. Stahl (1994, pp. 3–5) related that when students are given 3 seconds or more of undisturbed wait time, there are certain positive outcomes:

♦ The length and correctness of their responses increase.

♦ The number of "I don't know" and no-answer responses decreases.

♦ The number of volunteered, appropriate answers by larger numbers of students greatly increases.

♦ Students' scores on academic achievement tests tend to increase.

♦ When teachers wait patiently in silence for 3 seconds or more at appropriate places, positive changes in their own teacher behaviors also occur.

♦ Teachers' questioning strategies tend to be more varied and flexible.

♦ Teachers decrease the quantity and increase the quality and variety of their questions.

♦ Teachers ask additional questions that require more complex information processing and higher-level thinking on the part of students.

From the research of Stahl and others (e.g., Rowe, 1986), wait time is think time, and 3 seconds has been reported as the ideal amount of time to wait for student response.

FOCUS ON WAIT TIME

Observation focus: Wait time during class discussion or lecture.

Observation technique: Wide-angle approach that focuses on not so much the questions but the wait time between the time the teacher finishes the question and a student who is called on to answer the question.

Explanation of the tool and technique: Once the teacher completes articulating the question, track the wait time afforded before calling on a student to answer the question.

How and why the technique is helpful: This tool can help the teacher to focus on the amount of wait time between the question and the response while examining the complexity of questions. This type of data can help the teacher and observer examine student engagement, understanding of concepts, and the pace of questions asked.

Directions and approaches for using the tool: Using a watch with a second hand, note the time the teacher waits between completing the question and calling on a student. Note as much of the question as possible, focusing more on the end words of the question.

Tips

- Place your watch flat on the desk so that the teacher does not focus on you looking at the watch.
- Note as many questions as possible. It is more important to capture illustrative examples rather than every question the teacher asks.

Tool 17: Focus on Wait Time

Teacher: **Haidong Chen**   Date of Observation: **April 18, 2008**

Observer: **Francesca Duncan**

Class: **English I**   Period of the Day: **Period 1**

Time of Observation: Start: **8:05**   End: **8:20**

Total Time Spent in Observation: **15 minutes**

Number of Students Present: **24**   Grade Level: **Grade 9**

Topic of the Lesson: **S. E. Hinton's Rumble Fish**

Date of Postobservation Conference: **April 21, 2008**

Teacher Question	Wait Time (Seconds)
... in what year? ... James?	2 seconds
When you think of the lessons the characters learned by the end of the book, who do you think grew up the most?	3 seconds
How does the Siamese fighting fish come to be symbolic of the characters in this book?	5 seconds
Leslie, are there any other symbols?	4 seconds
Do these other symbols relate to the importance of the Siamese fighting fish?	2 seconds
Why do you suppose S. E. Hinton chose Siamese fighting fish rather than another type of domestic fish?	6 seconds

Another way to track wait time is to landscape data by including the taxonomy level of the questions related to wait time. This type of data can enhance analysis and reflection by examining both the type of questions using Bloom's Taxonomy and the amount of wait time (see Tool 18).

Tool 18: Wait Time With Bloom's Taxonomy for Examining Levels of Questions

Teacher: **Haidong Chen**   Date of Observation: **April 18, 2008**

Observer: **Francesca Duncan**

Class: **English I**   Period of the Day: **Period 1**

Time of Observation: Start: **8:05**   End: **8:20**

Total Time Spent in Observation: **15 minutes**

Number of Students Present: **24**   Grade Level: **Grade 9**

Topic of the Lesson: **S. E. Hinton's Rumble Fish**

Date of Postobservation Conference: **April 21, 2008**

Teacher Question	Wait Time (Seconds)	Question Domain
... in what year? ... James?	2 seconds	Knowledge
When you think of the lessons the characters learned by the end of the book, who do you think grew up the most?	3 seconds	Synthesis, Evaluation
How does the Siamese fighting fish come to be symbolic of the characters in this book?	5 seconds	Analysis
What deeper meanings can you apply to letting the fish out of their tanks at the end of the story?	3 seconds	Evaluation

Tips

♦ Suggest the teacher analyze wait time in terms of the type of question asked.

♦ Leave the "Question Domain" column blank and let the teacher fill in the level of taxonomy.

♦ If there is an overreliance on lower-level domains? Role-play with the teacher to rephrase the questions to move toward higher-order domains.

Suggested Postobservation Conference Strategies

Ms. Duncan prepared for the postobservation conference by thinking about the wait time in relation to the type of questions Mr. Chen asked. During the postobservation conference, Ms. Duncan

- ◆ invited Mr. Chen to review his questions and the amount of wait time he allowed;

- ◆ suggested that Mr. Chen analyze wait time in terms of the type of question asked, using Bloom's Taxonomy (Ms. Duncan had added an extra column to the observation form.); and

- ◆ encouraged Mr. Chen to determine if there were any other patterns to questions—more or less wait time during question groupings (e.g., Evaluation versus Knowledge).

Focus on Calling Patterns and Patterns of Interaction

Background

Teachers often wonder about their calling patterns. They want to know whom they are calling on and how often, whether they call on everyone, and whether they favor any one group of students or an area of the classroom. The patterns of interaction between a teacher and students are an essential part of the teaching and learning process.

Observation Focus: Calling and interaction patterns during a class period.

Observation Technique: Narrow Lens.

Explanation of the Tool and Technique: A narrow lens is used to track calling patterns—which students are engaging with the teacher. A seating chart is used to notate calling and interaction patterns.

How and Why the Technique is Helpful: Teachers can use the information to determine if they are calling on a variety of students, to see if any students are not participating, and to see if certain individuals are dominating class time.

Directions and Approaches for Using the Tool: Note the calling patterns (entire class responding, individual response, individual assistance, and so on). Develop a code for each. During the observation, track calling patterns on seating chart (Tool 19).

Tool 19: Tracking Calling Patterns

Teacher: **Susan Petrulis**   Date of Observation: **October 25, 2008**

Observer: **Francie Parker**

Class: **Social Studies**   Period of the Day: **4th period**

Time of Observation: Start: **11:00**   End: **11:20**

Total Time Spent in Observation: **20 Minutes**

Number of Students Present: **20**   Grade Level: **7th Grade**

Topic of the Lesson: **Vietnam War**

Date of Postobservation Conference: **October 27, 2008 (after school)**

Legend:

- ♦ Entire Class Response—ECR
- ♦ Individual Response—IR
- ♦ Individual Help—IH
- ♦ Question—Q
- ♦ Comment—C

Front of Room

	A	B	C	D
1.	CHARLES	JAMES 11:12-IR 11:16-IR 11:20-IR	MARY (sitting in back) 11:01-IR 11:05-Reading 11:12-IR	SAM 11:07-IR 11:10-Q 11:15-IH 11:18-IR
2.	CHRISTINE 11:10-Q to teacher 11:14-IR (w/repeat)	TONY 11:01-IR 11:02-C (we're good!) 11:10-IR	ANDREA Absent	RANDY 11:08-IR 11:09-Reading 11:20-IR
3.	MICHAEL	TIFFANY 11:04-IR 11:06-C	JEAN 11:00-C/R 11:11-IH 11:14-IR 11:18-C	SANDY

Tool continues on next page.

	A	B	C	D
4.	PATRICK Suspended	JEFF	KRISTY 11:03-Q 11:05-IH 11:13-IR	AMBER 11:14-C 11:17 -Q 11:18-Q
5.	ANDREW 11:07-IR 11:09-Read- ing 11:14 -IR	TYSON 11:04-C made by teacher 11:08-C 11:12-C		KATE Absent

Suggested Postobservation Conference Strategies

The data recorded on the chart enables the teacher to review her own calling patterns (frequency, gender, and so forth). Lead the teacher through examining the calling patterns as portrayed in Tool 20 on the next page.

ALTERNATE APPROACH TO
COLLECTING DATA RELATED TO CALLING PATTERNS

Tool 20:   Tracking Calling Patterns—Seating Chart*

The following approach focuses broadly on the distribution of calling patterns across boys and girls.

Teacher: **Susan Petrulis**   Date of Observation: **October 27, 2008**

Observer: **Francie Parker**

Class: **Social Studies**   Period of the Day: **4th period**

Time of Observation: Start: **11:00**   End: **11:20**

Total Time Spent in Observation: **20 Minutes**

Number of Students Present: **20**   Grade Level: **7th Grade**

Topic of the Lesson: **Vietnam War**

Date of Postobservation Conference: **October 27, 2008 (after school)**

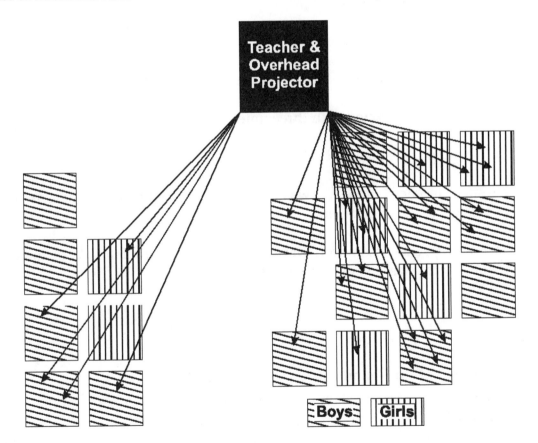

---

*This tool was developed by Meredith A. Byrd, Clayton County Public Schools (Jonesboro, GA).

Suggested Postobservation Conference Strategies

The patterns as depicted in the following analysis will lead to follow-up questions. Teaching is full of blind spots, such as avoiding certain areas of the classroom, overcalling on certain students such as those who are easily distracted, and, in some cases, calling on more boys than girls or girls than boys. The key is to help the teacher "see" the patterns that emerge in the data.

Analysis

- 20 students in the classroom

  - 7 female and 13 male

    - 9 questions directed to females

  - All 7 females were interacted with

    - 9 students interacted with one time

    - 5 students interacted with two times

    - 1 student interacted with three times

    - 1 student interacted with four times

  - 19.2% of teacher interaction was directed to the right side of the class-room which consisted of 7 students

  - 80.8% of teacher interaction was directed towards the left side of the class-room which consisted of 13 students

Tips

- Record events in 5-minute intervals.
- Record enough information so that the teacher can make sense of the overall events of the classroom.
- Include verbal statements as necessary to focus conversation during follow-up with the teacher.
- Avoid making value judgments while chronicling what is observed.

CAUSE AND EFFECT

Background

Classrooms are highly interactive environments. Examining cause and effect can help teachers examine the effect that their words and actions have on students. This process works in reverse, as well; the actions and words of students can have an effect on what teachers do and say.

Observation focus: Tracking teacher behaviors to determine the effects they have on students.

Observation technique: Wide-angle lens technique that examines teachers' actions and words and the effects they have on students.

Explanation of the tool and technique: This tool is designed to give the principal and the teacher information concerning the influence of the teacher's actions on students' responses in the classroom. This tool can be useful in observing a teacher's classroom management, direction giving, and other teacher behaviors related to student response.

How and why the technique is helpful: This type of information can be especially helpful for new teachers or teachers who are experiencing difficulties with classroom management (student behavior, managing learning activities, and transitions). This tool gives the teacher information about the influence of the teacher's actions on student responses. This tool can be useful in observing a teacher's classroom management, questioning strategies, direction giving, and other teacher behaviors that ask for a student response.

Directions and approaches for using the tool: Divide a blank sheet of paper into two columns. Record teacher actions in the left-hand column and record student responses to these actions in the right-hand column.

Tip

♦ Focus on concrete actions, directions, or words of the teacher and the subsequent behavior of students.

Tool 21: Cause and Effect

Teacher: **James Ackman**   Date of Observation: **May 5, 2008**

Observer: **Juanita Powell**

Class: **Accounting I**   Period of the Day: **6th period**

Time of Observation: Start: **1:15**   End: **1:35**

Total Time Spent in Observation: **20 minutes**

Number of Students Present: **26**   Grade level: **Mixed (Juniors and Seniors)**

Topic of the Lesson: **Using Accounting Software**

Date of Postobservation Conference: **May 6, 2008**

Time	Teacher	Student Response or Activity
Bell (1:15)	At desk organizing papers	Milling around room
1:15–1:21	Takes roll Makes announcements Collects homework	Quietly talking
1:22	Turns on overhead and says, "Take out your notebooks and open your book to page 140."	Students pull out materials. Red shirt slapping boy next to him (Blue shirt)
1:23	"Folks, heads up to the overhead and focus on the chapter objectives." Begins stating the objectives for the chapter.	Shuffling to get their books out and open to page 140. Seven students (out of 16) do not have books.
1:19–1:23	"Read from pages 140 to 145." Teacher sitting at desk getting software to boot up for a demonstration	Students without books: Two are talking with each other Two are sleeping Three are reading from nearby student's books
1:24	"Who would like to offer a summary while I get the program loaded?"	Four students are still reading; three students (who did not have book) are talking with their neighbors; two students sleeping; four students raise their hands; one student asks a question out loud, "How can you expect us to finish reading five pages in 10 minutes," and another student blurts, "Bite me."

Tool continues on next page.

Time	Teacher	Student Response or Activity
1:26	"James, repeat what you said."	James: "Bite me."
1:27	"James, I just cannot believe you said, 'bite me' Are you talking to me?"	Yeah, yeah, just "get bit," Ackman.
1:28	Pushes the call button for assistance.	Eight students talking; three laughing, James walks to the door
1:29	Loading computer program	Students are talking among themselves.
1:30	Announces: Technology is not cooperating today. Pull out books and look at the study questions at the end of the chapter	Students pull out books and start to thumb through the chapter.

Suggested Postobservation Conference Strategies

Ask the teacher to examine the data. Ask probing questions related to the timing of events, how words led to escalating the events of the verbal exchange. Brainstorm with the teacher about other strategies that might have caused a different outcome. Topical areas could include the use of activities or strategies while the computer program was loading.

VARIETY OF INSTRUCTIONAL METHODS

Background

Regardless of subject area, grade level, or the teacher's experience, a single class period should include a variety of instructional methods. Research has cast new light on the way children learn, and can we no longer assume that any one instructional strategy is sufficient to reach *all* learners *all* of the time. Effective teachers not only use a variety of instructional strategies but also differentiate strategies. To differentiate, teachers provide alternative approaches to the methods used to present content and the ways that students show mastery of learning objectives. Given the myriad ability levels of students and the recognition that no two learners learn at the same rate or in the same way, differentiated instruction shows great promise as a way of thinking about teaching and learning. In a classroom in which instruction is differentiated, students are offered a variety of ways to learn. According to Tomlinson (1999, p. 2), differentiated instruction flourishes when the following occur:

- Teachers begin where the students are;
- Teachers engage students in instruction through different learning modalities;
- Students compete more against themselves than against others;
- Teachers provide specific ways for each individual to learn;
- Teachers use classroom time flexibly; and
- Teachers are diagnosticians, prescribing the best possible instruction for each student.

Observation focus: Variety of instructional techniques.

Observation technique: Narrow-angle lens technique focusing on the number of instructional strategies, the length of each, and the activities students engage in during each.

Explanation of the tool and technique: For each instructional strategy used, indicate the time and what the teacher and the students are doing. Additional information such as transitions could also be noted. Tracking variety of instructional strategies will require a longer classroom observation, perhaps an entire class period; however, it is not outside of the realm of possibility for the principal to observe in a classroom where more than one instructional technique is used in a 15–20 minute span of time.

How and why the technique is helpful: This technique can give insight about the number and duration of instructional strategies used during a class segment.

Tips

- Note teacher cues for each strategy and the transitions between methods or activities used to further the methods.
- Note the length of each strategy.

Tool 22: Variety of Instructional Materials

Teacher: **Shelly Beter**　　　　　Date of Observation: **March 4, 2008**

Observer: **Julie Escobar**

Class: **English I (Remedial)**　　　Period of the Day: **Block 1**

Time of Observation:　Start: **9:00**　　End: **9:25**

Total Time Spent in Observation: **25 minutes**

Number of Students Present: **25**　　Grade Level: **9th grade**

Topic of the Lesson: **S. E. Hinton's Rumble Fish**

Date of Postobservation Conference: **March 4, 2008**

Time	Instructional Method	Teacher Behavior	Student Activities
9:00–9:05	Organizing lecture	Lecturing, Q & A period about plot Distributes an index card to each student: Directs students to write one sentence about the importance of the Siamese fighting fish	Listening, taking notes, Asking questions
9:06–9:08	Independent work	Monitoring student work	Students write on the index cards
9:09–9:22	Large-group sharing	Teacher seeks volunteers to share insights about the Siamese fighting fish and its importance thus far in the book; asking for "proofs" from the text to support ideas written on the index cards Leading students to citations offered by groups	Sharing thoughts about the symbol of the Siamese fighting fish; finding citations from the text to support ideas;
9:23–9:25	Question and answer	Asking questions	Responding to questions (looking up citations to back up ideas); asking questions

Suggested Postobservation Conference Strategies

Later the same day, Julie Escobar visited Shelly Beter for a few minutes and asked her to review the observation notes so she could analyze the data on her own. The next day, Julie and Shelly met before school to discuss the classroom observation. Julie began the conversation with an open-ended question, "What patterns do you see?"

During the postobservation conference, Julie and Shelly reviewed the various instructional strategies used, the amount of time spent on each, what students were doing during each, and what learning objectives were being met. On reflection, Shelly shared that she really did not give students enough time to write out ideas and concepts on the note cards and that she would experiment with (1) extending the amount of time for note taking and (2) giving more explicit directions to students prior to having them work independently. She shared that some students were still having difficulties with finding "proofs" from the text of the novel.

EXAMINING TEACHER–STUDENT DISCUSSION WITH A FOCUS ON HOW STUDENT COMMENTS ARE INCORPORATED INTO THE LESSON

Background

Nothing keeps a class moving forward more than a lively discussion in which student responses are incorporated into the lesson. Teachers who incorporate student responses into lessons extend learning and are able to check more readily for understanding. Student responses also serve to assess student learning, giving cues to the connections students are making with content, their ability to apply what they are learning, and the areas that need to be reinforced or retaught. When a teacher incorporates student comments, such behavior signals a student-centered classroom in which student questions often serve to extend the concepts that are being studied.

Observation focus: Incorporating student comments and ideas into the discussion.

Observation technique: Narrow focus using selective verbatim.

Explanation of the tool and technique: This tool is designed to give the principal and the teacher information concerning how teachers incorporate student comments into class discussions.

How and why the technique is helpful: This technique can also help teachers to assess student learning based on student responses and to become aware of the information student responses can give relative to understanding and application of concepts previously taught.

Directions and approaches for using the tool: Note what the teacher says (focusing on questions), the student response to the question, and then what the teacher does with the student response.

Tip

- ♦ Given the fast nature of classroom discussions, writing question stems will suffice (e.g., "Can we find examples from the text …").

Tool 23:   Examining Teacher–Student Discussion With a Focus on How Student Comments Are Incorporated Into the Lesson

Teacher: **Jack Howard**   Date of Observation: **April 28, 2008**

Observer: **Jeannette Geter**

Class: **English I**   Period of the Day: **2nd period**

Time of Observation: Start: **8:50**   End: **9:06**

Total Time Spent in Observation: **16 minutes**

Number of Students Present: **25**   Grade Level: **9th grade (Honors)**

Topic of the Lesson: **Symbolism found in S. E. Hinton's Rumble Fish**

Date of Postobservation Conference: **April 29, 2008**

Time	Teacher Talk/Question	Student Response	How Student Comments Are Used
8:50	A symbol is an object that represents something else. What are the symbols in Rumble Fish?	SR1: Siamese rumble fish	Can you expand on this? (Mr. Howard asks)
		SR2: The gangs are made up of people who can't get along with one another	Cite an example of this from the text?
8:53		SR3: See page 47.	Relate this to the end of the book
8:55		SR4: At the end, the Siamese fighting fish are let go.	Does this parallel the death of the character?
8:57	In your opinion, was letting the fish go an act of bravery?	SR5: He was making a statement about being free ... on page 98 it says he was born in the wrong era	OK, but was this act bravery or an act of cowardice?

Tool continues on next page.

Time	Teacher Talk/Question	Student Response	How Student Comments Are Used
9:01			What do you think the narrator meant by the "wrong era?"
		SR6: He just did not fit into the world he lives	What made him an outcast?
9:06	Can we find examples from the text that back up the idea he did not fit into the world he lives?		

Suggested Postobservation Conference Strategies

This data collection tool allows the principal to capture how the teacher incorporates student responses into the overall lecture and classroom discussion. Jeannette spends a few minutes having Jack look at what he did with student responses. To do this, Jeannette encouraged Jack to track the type of responses students gave and what he did to incorporate student responses into the discussion.

Jeannette then encouraged Jack to

1. track what strategies he used while incorporating comments.
2. examine the types of questions he used to extend student thinking. Jack used Bloom's Taxonomy and then he examined whether or not his questions were "open-ended" so that students could branch out into other related areas of the book.
3. Jeannette asked Jack the following questions:
    ♦ Have students expanded on each other's ideas?
    ♦ Did students look up information in the book to support answers?
    ♦ Did students write their ideas in notebooks?

FOCUS ON TRACKING TRANSITION PATTERNS

Background

The transition is, in a sense, an instructional method. Smooth transitions conserve time, help to keep students focused on learning objectives, and lessen opportunities for classroom disruptions. Transitions are enhanced when materials are assembled in advance, lessening the loss of time between activities and allowing smoother movement from one method of instruction to another. Transitions are seamless, with students assuming some responsibility for efficient operation. Transitions are more successful when teachers do the following:

♦ Establish and reinforce routines;
♦ Cue students to a transition so they are ready to transition to the next activity;
♦ Provide clear directions as part of the transition; and
♦ Have materials available before the transition begins.

Observation focus: Transition strategies

Observation technique: Narrow angle focusing only on the transitions that a teacher uses between activities or instructional segments

Explanation of the tool and technique: The principal tracks which techniques the teacher uses between instructional segments—that is, how the teacher gets students from point A to point B.

How and why this technique is helpful: This technique helps the teacher to examine how activities and instruction are organized and the amount of time it takes to move from one activity to another. For teachers who might be having difficulty with student behavior, this strategy can assist teachers in improving their classroom-management.

Directions and approaches for using the tool: Record broadly the instructional activity and then the transition (cues, clarity of directions) used to move students from one activity to another, focusing on student responses based on the transition strategy.

Tool 24: Focus on Tracking Transition Patterns

Teacher: **Cheryl Hofer**   Date of Observation: **January 18, 2008**

Observer: **June Kaufman**

Class: **3rd grade (Math)**   Period of the Day: **Morning**

Time of Observation: Start: **10:10**   End: **10:24**

Total Time Spent in Observation: **14 minutes**

Number of Students Present: **18**   Grade Level: **4th grade**

Topic of the Lesson: **Map activity—geography**

Date of Postobservation Conference: **January 22, 2008**

Instruction/Activity	Transition	Student Response
10:10–10:14: Getting students into cooperative groups	Gives directions for small cooperative group. Stops movement to give clarifying instructions. Hands out worksheets, maps, and other supplies.	Students meander, finding their group members; four students ask clarifying questions during movement.
	Teacher directs team captains to pick up direction sheet for their groups.	
	Materials are packaged on teacher's desk; packets have a number on them corresponding to the group (e.g., 1, 2, 3). Captains pick up packet.	Two groups did not know who was the designated captain.
10:15–10:24: Students are working in groups. Teacher is walking from group to group redirecting students, answering questions.		

Tool continues on next page.

Instruction/Activity	Transition	Student Response
10:20: Teacher reminds students that they have four minutes left to complete task.		Students continue to work; one group has completed the map—members are checking accuracy of sign markers.
10:24: Getting students back into large group	Flicks lights on and off, asks Group 1 to send their rep to the front of the room to give a summary.	Students are moving desks back into rows and getting ready for whole-class work.

Suggested Postobservation Conference Strategies

Encourage the teacher to examine the transitions and how students respond throughout the transition periods. Suggest that the teacher examine the minutes involved in the transition, the directions or cues, and how students respond to these directions and cues.

TRACKING STUDENT BEHAVIOR

Background

Tracking student behavior helps teachers who are experiencing classroom-management issues, regardless of the teacher's experience level. However, observing student behavior is not necessarily related to discipline issues. Teachers establish classroom routines, plan lessons, organize materials, and interact with students with the best of intentions. Teachers can benefit from data about student behavior to pinpoint areas to be more aware of as they manage instruction, learning objectives, activities, and interactions with students. Data that clearly focus on student behavior and classroom- and instructional-management techniques can yield a fuller understanding of the complexities of teaching.

Observation focus: Student behavior.

Observation technique: Narrow focus broadly applied to tracking student behavior during instruction—directions, verbal and nonverbal cues from the teacher and student response.

Explanation of the tool and technique: This tool will help the observer to focus on teacher behaviors and their effect on student behavior and response.

How and why the technique is helpful: With the fast-paced nature of instruction, sometimes teachers cannot readily analyze the effect their words have on student behavior. This tool can assist the teacher in analyzing what is said and how students respond to what is being said, in addition to overall classroom management.

Directions and approaches for using the tool: Track teacher behavior (words, routines, activities, directions, etc.) and then immediately note student behavior.

Tip

♦ Encourage the teacher to look for patterns in student behaviors.

Tool 25:   Tracking Student Behavior

Teacher: **Samuel Ortiz**   Date of Observation: **May 6, 2008**

Observer: **Martin Scott**

Class: **6th grade**   Period of the Day: **Afternoon**

Time of Observation: Start: **2:20**   End: **2:35**

Total Time Spent in Observation: **15 minutes**

Number of Students Present: **18**   Grade level: **6th grade**

Topic of the Lesson: **Language arts (Verbs)**

Date of Postobservation Conference: **May 7, 2008**

	Teacher	&		Student
1 2:20	Look at the Word of the Day on the board and write a sentence using the word. The word today is "catastrophe."	1		Just one sentence or two?
2 2:20	One sentence, like we do every day.	2		We didn't do a word yesterday.
3 2:20	OK, then, like the one we did a few days ago.	3		
4 2:21	Tom, read your sentence.	4		I'm not done ... I came in late.
5 2:22	Randy, let's hear your sentence.	5		My pen is out of ink ... I can say the sentence I would have written.
6 2:22	Randy, this is the third time this week you have not come to class prepared to work.	6		Yeah, yeah, yeah.I only have pencils.
7 2:22	That's right ... you can only use a pen to write class notes.	7		I don't like pens ... you can't erase the marks.
8 2:23	Pens are what you must use ... What don't you understand about this?	8		Why can't I use a pencil...But Mrs. Elbertson lets us use pencils ... so do all my teachers, but you.

Tool continues on next page.

	Teacher	&	Student
9 2:23	That's right, young man, young stand out in the hall for the next 15 minutes. Go to the office … now.	9	
10 2:24	Does anyone want to read their sentence?	10	Three hands go up
11 2:25	Leslie, go ahead and read your sentence.	11	After several attempts, the sailors were able to avoid a catastrophe at sea.
12 2:25	Excellent sentence, Leslie.	12	
13 2:26	Pull out your grammar your books and go to page 89. Make sure your notebooks are ready for class notes.	13	Students begin to pull out books from book bags. Two students (girls in third row, far right) begin to pull at a book); students to their right exchange books and a notebook.
14 2:29	Go to Sentence 5, "The children seated at the table began asking for dessert." Look at the word "seated." Can this word be the verb in this sentence?	14	Hands go up, teacher asks Joey (his hand not raised) to answer the question. Laughter with other hands starting to go up.
15 2:29	Joey, what is your answer?	15	Yes.
16 2:29	Why all the laughter? And Joey, look at the sentence again.	16	
17 2:30	What is a participle?	17	About nine hands go up; four students looking in book for the answer; five students looking around the room.
18 2:31	Anna	18	A word that ends in "ed," "en," "n," or "ing."
19 2:31		19	Boy shouts out "Not!"

Tool continues on next page.

	Teacher	*&*	*Student*
20 2:32	Tony, why "not"	20	What about "the man died"—isn't died a verb in that sentence and it ends in "ed"? Students in the third row are talking.
21 2:33	That's right in the Sentence Tony gave. you. But look back at Sentence 5 ... The word is "seated." The word "seated" is really functioning as what? Teacher does not call on students to answer ... He begins to "teach" Let's consider a few points: ♦ Pure grammatical rules do not always apply—you have to look at the sentence and how each word is being used. ♦ A participle is more than a word that has a certain ending. A participle is usually a multiworded adjective ... ♦ Let's look at the proof to determine if a word is an adjective.	21	Hands fly up ... students want to answer ... they are making sounds (ooh, ooh, ohh).
22 2:35	What is the proof to see if a word is an adjective?	22	Jackson answers: Whose, which, what kind of, how many.

Suggested Postobservation Conference Strategies

Martin leaves his observation notes with Samuel so he can examine the data. When Martin and Sam meet the next day, Martin opens the discussion with the question, "How do you think things went in class yesterday with this group of students?" There is a long pause, and Samuel admits he needs help with this group of students. Martin agrees, and he thinks the best way to proceed is to have Samuel identify the patterns in classroom routines, student response patterns, and how Samuel responds to students. From these patterns, Martin and Samuel are in a position to start reconstructing the events and develop alternate strategies to focus students.

CLASSROOM TRAFFIC

Background

The classroom is often marked by the movement of teachers and their physical proximity with students. Movement could include movement during a lecture, while checking on student progress during independent work or work in cooperative groups, and during demonstrations. Because of content, some classes require more movement for teachers and students. Think of the fast-paced nature of instruction in the gym, a consumer science course (sewing or foods lab), a band or choral room, and even the "traditional classroom" where demonstrations occur. Teachers seek feedback regarding their own movement and often the movement of their students. Teachers may wonder if there are any "blind" spots, or areas of the classroom in which students are not being attended to during the instructional period. Tracking classroom traffic gives teachers insight on their movements during class.

Observation focus: Teacher movement around the room and contact with students.

Observation technique: Narrow lens.

Explanation of the tool and technique: This tool allows the principal to track the movement of the teacher and/or students during an observation. Using a seating chart, the principal uses lines to track these movements.

How and why the technique is helpful: The teacher and the principal will be able to recreate the movement throughout the time in which the observation occurs.

Directions and approaches for using the tool: On a seating chart (Tool 26 on next page), use lines to track the movement of the teacher. Notate times along the lines so that not only the movement but the length of time the teacher works with each student can be tracked as well.

Tool 26: Classroom Traffic—Seating Chart

Teacher: **Shirley West**   Date of Observation: **April 28, 2008**

Observer: **Paula Aguilar**

Class: **Algebra II**   Period of the Day: **1st Hour**

Time of Observation: Start: **7:45**   End: **8:00**

Total Time Spent in Observation: **15 Minutes**

Number of Students Present: **18**   Grade Level: **Mixed 10th and 11th**

Topic of the Lesson: **Hyperbolas—How to graph and write equations of hyperbolas that consist of two vaguely parabola-shaped pieces that open either up or down**

Date of Postobservation Conference: **April 29, 2008**

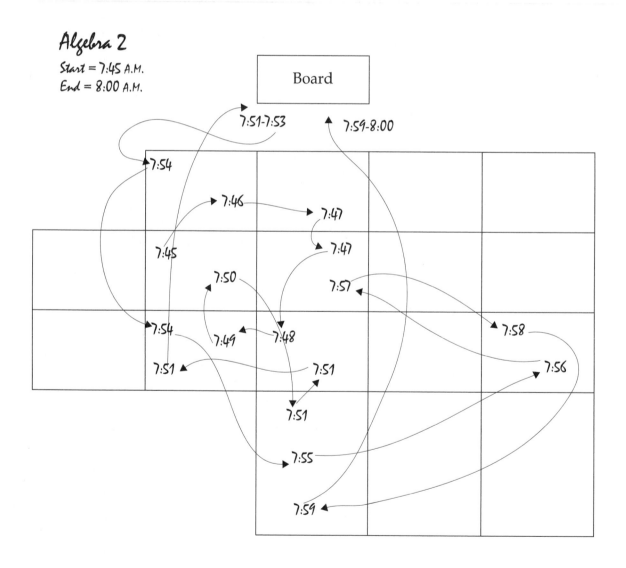

Tips

+ To reduce the amount of "noise" on any one diagram, use more than one seating chart for an extended classroom observation, notating the start and end time at the top of each.

+ Record anecdotal notes in the margins or on another sheet of paper.

Suggested Postobservation Conference Strategies

With the seating chart as a backdrop for the postobservation conference, lead the teacher into "seeing" the patterns of movement. Probing questions could include the following:

+ Which students did you spend a majority of the time working with?
+ Were there students who did not need assistance?

TRACKING THE BEGINNING AND ENDING (CLOSURE) OF CLASS

Background

Effective teachers engage in bell-to-bell instruction. The first few minutes and the last few minutes are acknowledged as two critically important points of time. Research shows that time wasted at the beginning and ending of class can never really be recouped; once time is lost, it is gone. Effective teachers establish daily routines for beginning and ending class. Grade level dictates the types of routines established. Although there are vast differences among elementary, middle, and high school classrooms, all share a commonality: the need for routines to begin and end instruction.

Beginning Class Routines

Teachers who have routines for the beginning of a class period use the time immediately before the tardy bell for getting students ready and organized for learning. Strategies to maximize time on task and to reduce "empty air time" before formal instruction begin include the following:

+ taking attendance as students are entering the room;
+ having a "sponge" activity, such as a short quiz or math problem, for students to start working on as they arrive;

- posting they day's agenda and what materials to get ready before the bell rings; and
- distributing class materials and collecting homework.

All of these activities help to prepare students so that the moment the bell rings, instruction or other activities related to the lesson can begin.

Ending Class Routines

Effective teachers use the time immediately before the ending of a class period to review lessons learned and to help bring closure to the class activities. They relate what needs to be done to prepare for the next day so that once the bell rings, students can be dismissed. Different cues give students time to put away supplies and equipment and get ready to leave the class in an orderly manner.

Tracking the Beginning of Class

Observation focus: Activities within the first 15 minutes of class beginning or the last 15 minutes of the class.

Observation technique: Narrow focus using anecdotal notes.

Explanation of the tool and technique: The principal will want to examine the routines used to begin or to come to closure of the class.

How and why this technique is helpful: This anecdotal technique allows the observer to chronicle activities that support bell-to-bell instruction at two key times during the class period—the beginning and ending of the instructional period. This technique focuses data collection on the events and instructional activities either the beginning or the ending of the period to assess how time is being used to focus student learning.

Directions and approaches for using the tool: Chronicle the activities and procedures the teacher uses to begin or to end class instruction. Note the amount of time it takes the teacher to open or close class, paying particular attention to the routines, student familiarity with routines, and the cues the teacher uses to signal students.

Tips

- Record data in 1- and 1-minute increments.
- Record major events in detail. A few strong examples with complete and accurate information will make more sense than trying to record extraneous information.
- Leave a space such as a large column in the margin to be used during the postobservation conference to make notes (e.g., teacher analysis, questions, concerns, or ideas).

Tool 27: Beginning of Class Routines

Teacher: **Amy Kleibar** Date of Observation: **May 6, 2008**

Observer: **Sou Chen**

Class: **English I** Period of the Day: **Period 1**

Time of Observation: Start: **8:05** End: **8:20**

Total Time Spent in Observation: **15 minutes**

Number of Students Present: **23** Grade Level: **9th grade**

Topic of the Lesson: **(NA due to focus on beginning of class routines)**

Date of Postobservation Conference: **May 7, 2008**

	Beginning of the Period	*Student Behavior*
8:05	Attendance taken as students enter the room. Teacher [T] in the doorway stopping students as they enter reminding students to take off coats and hats.	Students entering the room and stopping by T's desk to pick up graded papers; students comparing grades as they walk to their desks (clusters of students clog the doorway and area around T's desk).
8:07	Bell rings. Teacher closes door and picks up papers left on desk—calls students up to the front of the room to pick up papers.	Students sitting at desk while T gives students their papers; student in row 3 trips a student; two students in row 5 push around books while walking up the aisles.
8:08	Announcements from the activities office; opens the door for late students; stops at the computer station to log tardy students.	Students sitting at desk: nine students turned around talking to other students during announcements; five students are digging materials out from their book bags; three students lined up at the pencil sharpener.
8:11	Teacher cues students to review due dates for next essay—points to the board and tells students, "Get these dates in notebooks."	Students start opening notebooks … three are trying to borrow paper (no notebooks).

Tool continues on next page.

		Beginning of the Period	*Student Behavior*
8:12		Teacher cues students, "Review my comments on your papers. Revisions are due tomorrow—rewrite only the parts of the essay circled in green."	Students start thumbing through essays ... one student asks what to do if there are no "green circles." Lots of laughter.
8:13		Teacher cue: "It's a bit noisy in here today ... Let's begin by reviewing the elements of an introductory paragraph, but first pull out Writing Tip Sheet 3 from your writing folders ...	Students begin looking in book bags for writing folders ... several begin to move closer to one another ...
8:14		Teacher offers copies of Writing Tip Sheet to three students who do not have this sheet ... gives out sheet to 13 students	A student asks, "Are we going to finish our group activity from yesterday?"
8:14		Teacher: First, we're going to review the elements of an introductory paragraph ... review silently for a moment the key elements of an introductory paragraph ...	Students start to read the sheet.
8:15		Teacher walks around the room as students read Writing Tip Sheet	Students are quietly reading sheet.
8:18		Teacher turns on overhead ... overhead has a sample introductory paragraph written by the student who had "no green circles" on his paper ... teacher cues students to the paragraph and asks them to (1) read the paragraph, (2) compare the elements of an introductory paragraph to the sample on the overhead, and (3) write a few thoughts about the sample paragraph related to the elements found on Tip Sheet 3.	Students focus on the paragraph quietly reading it ... many students are writing notes in notebook ... a few students are talking with their neighbors ... talk is quiet.
8:19–8:20		Teacher is walking around the room monitoring.	

Suggested Postobservation Conference Strategies

Lead the teacher through looking for patterns in:

♦ traffic patterns before the start bell rings;
♦ routines for getting started;
♦ student familiarity with routines; and
♦ verbal and nonverbal cues the teacher gives to students.

Tracking End of Class Routines

The next tool helps the principal to collect data toward the end of an instructional period.

Tool 28: Tracking End of Class Routines

Teacher: **Amy Kleibar**   Date of Observation: **May 6, 2008**

Observer: **Sou Chen**

Class: **English I**   Period of the Day: **Period 1**

Time of Observation: Start: **8:45**   End: **9:00**

Total Time Spent in Observation: **15 minutes**

Number of Students Present: **23**   Grade Level: **9th grade**

Topic of the Lesson: **Focus on ending of class routines**

Date of Postobservation Conference: **May 7, 2008**

	Ending of the Period	*Student Behavior*
8:45	Teacher is moving from group to group, speaking with students, examining work ...	Students are in small groups Discussing essays.
8:48	Teacher cues students to move desks back in place for large-group processing.	Students start to break out of groups by moving desks back in rows ... minimal noise ... a student from each group is putting books (thesaurus, dictionary, etc.) back on teacher's desk.
8:49	Teacher is in front of the room readying for instruction ... makes a few statements: (1) Please bring notebooks tomorrow, and I'll add more information about the essay. (2) Also, rewrites on the areas circled in green are due tomorrow, just rewrite the sections circled in green.	Student desks are in a row and students are listening to the teacher, quietly.
8:50	Let's recap the importance of the advanced organizer in the introductory paragraph and how this organizer serves as a transition to subsequent paragraphs ...	Students sit quietly for about 10 seconds ... hands start going up...

Tool continues on next page.

	Ending of the Period	*Student Behavior*
8:50	Jamie ...	The organizer is the road map and helps the writer point to the major points that get discussed in the essay ... in a way it's a writer's compass ...
8:51	That's an interesting metaphor ... a compass ... is there any other value to a compass?	Fred responds, the organizer is for the reader, too ... the compass helps the traveler know what direction he is in ... going ...
8:52	Excellent parallel ... let's look at a sample from an essay ... teacher flips the overhead on and focuses students to the advanced organizer sentence that is in all bold on the screen ... look at this advanced organizer ... comment on its importance and value ... Lauren ... what do you think?	Lauren responds ... this organizer has three items in it ... the symbols in the book 1. help to illustrate the deeper meaning, 2. provide an understanding of the what motivated the main character, and 3. foreshadow the ending of the book.
8:54	Superb ... now what does the writer need to do next ...	Several hands go up ...
8:55	Jackson ... what do you think?	"Take time to write another sentence or two ... the organizer acts as a segue to the next paragraphs ... Student asks a question, does the advanced organizer have to always have three points?"
8:56	Actually, the number of points is not important because...	Student responds...it depends on what the essay is trying to get across ...
8:56	That's correct ... And we'll be reviewing several more introductory paragraphs tomorrow ... let's recap from the day ... teacher highlights the *Tips for Writing Introductory* paragraphs, the uses and misuses of advanced organizer and the purpose of the advanced organizer.	Students are listening and taking notes ... three students are starting to pack up their materials ... teacher cues disapproval by standing by the desk of one student ... the others stop packing up their materials ...

Tool continues on next page.

	Ending of the Period	*Student Behavior*
9:00	Bell rings and teacher thanks the class for working hard and wishes them well for the rest of the day.	Students pack up their bags and start leaving the room.

Suggested Postobservation Conference Strategies

Lead the teacher through looking for patterns in:

♦ Student familiarity with closure routines;

♦ Verbal and nonverbal cues the teacher gives to students;

♦ Use of strategies to summarize and come to closure; and

♦ Orderly dismissal.

COOPERATIVE LEARNING GROUPS

Background

Cooperative learning is an instructional model in which students complete work collaboratively in small groups. The work of a cooperative learning group is structured so that each group member contributes to the completion of the learning activity. Cooperative learning group work is sometimes chaotic, with students talking with one another, perhaps even across groups, comparing answers, quizzing one another, or securing materials from bookshelves. In cooperative learning, students assume a variety of active roles including, leader, time keeper, runner, recorder, and presenter. Because the cooperative learning structures encourage not only the content of what is being learned but also social and leadership skills, the teacher encourages students to rotate roles. Figure 4.2 outlines common roles that students assume in cooperative learning structures and the tasks of the student assuming these roles.

Because the work of the student who is the recorder is different from the work of the student who assumes the role of runner, the principal needs to realize that students in cooperative learning groups are engaged in a variety of ways doing things differently throughout the duration of the group's time together. Observing in a classroom using cooperative group structures will look very different in a classroom where the teacher is lecturing, for example.

Teaching in a cooperative group structure looks different. The directions the teacher provides, the monitoring the teacher does within and across groups, and the eye to time on task are essential for cooperative learning to be successful. In cooperative learning, the teacher assumes responsibility for monitoring students' learning and intervening within the groups, and teaching begins well before the class meets.

Figure 4.2. Cooperative Learning Roles

Role	Tasks
Leader	Ensures all group members have the opportunity to participate fully; focuses discussions and activities around the primary group task.
Time Keeper	Keeps an eye on the clock, keeping members on task; gives the group reminders at mid-point and ending points of time left to accomplish tasks.
Runner	Ensures the group has materials to accomplish tasks; at peak times leaves the group to get materials or to ask the teacher for assistance or clarification.
Recorder	Records the group's work—keeps track of key ideas.
Presenter	Presents the group's work to larger group.

Depending on when the principal enters the room, a variation on data collection includes using anecdotal notes across the categories that Johnson and Johnson (1994) identified as essential to framing cooperative learning. The following data-collection tool (Tool 29) can help the principal script anecdotal notes while observing in a classroom where cooperative learning is being used.

Tool 29: Focus on Cooperative Learning

Focus	Notes
Objectives for the cooperative learning group	*Objectives for the lesson were on the board with direction for students to form groups.*
Clarity of directions	*Teacher restated the directions before students moved to groups.*
Transitions from small to large group work	*Teacher cued the students with "two minutes left!"*
Monitoring and intervening strategies	*Teacher walking around the room and moved from group to group.*
Evaluation strategies	*N/A*
Interactions with students	*Called students by name; very respectful.*
Follow-up instruction	*N/A*

Observation focus: Student interaction and teacher monitoring.

Observation technique: Narrow lens focusing on the work of students in groups and the teacher's monitoring strategies.

Explanation of the tool and technique: The cooperative learning model is dependent on small-group work. This tool will assist in tracking not only the work of students but also how a teacher attends to the work of students in small groups.

How and why the technique is helpful: Through monitoring the group activities, the teacher will be able to determine individual student involvement (Johnson & Johnson, 1994). The principal can assist teachers in assessing the work of students, individually or in groups, by collecting data on what students are doing and how students are interacting with one another in cooperative learning groups.

Directions and approaches for using the tool: Once students are in groups, record the interactions of students and the strategies the teacher uses to monitor the work of students within groups.

Tips

♦ Track teacher movement from group to group.

♦ Record teacher verbal cues such as directions for the groups prior to and during cooperative group activities.

♦ Depending on the situation, the principal should feel free to walk around the room to be able to hear students interact with one another and to hear teacher's cues redirecting student focus, and to get a better sense of what strategies the teacher uses to intervene in the work of small groups.

Tool 30: Cooperative Learning—
Student Interactions and Teacher Monitoring

Teacher: **Theresa Lipinski**   Date of Observation: **April 30, 2008**

Observer: **Carol Overman**

Class: **English 1**   Period of the Day: **7th period**

Time of observation: Start: **1:50**   End: **2:10**

Total Time Spent in Observation: **20 minutes**

Number of Students Present: **23**   Grade Level: **Freshman (Honors)**

Topic of the Lesson: **Romeo and Juliet**

Date of Postobservation Conference: **May 1, 2008**

Group	Number in Group	Student Interaction	Teacher Monitoring Strategies
1	4	Discussing the use of foreshadowing—one student recording comments; one student finding supporting citations from the text; two students talking with one another	Teacher with Group 4
2	3	Two students reading book, scanning for citations—no talking; one student sketching a crest for the Montague family	Teacher physically with Group 4 but "eye scanning" Group 5
3	4	One student asking questions—one student writing responses—one student doodling in notebook (Capulet crest)—one student reading biology book	Teacher moves to Group 5— teacher speaking with group members—full attention to Group 5
4	4	Students reading text and alternately speaking with one another ... one student starts to draw the family crest for the Capulets	Teacher stays with Group 5 for 4 minutes

Tool continues on next page.

Group	Number in Group	Student Interaction	Teacher Monitoring Strategies
5	4	Two students talking loudly; one student looking in book bag; one student talking to a student in Group 6	Teacher "making eye contact" from position in with Group 4 ... teacher breaks in with an announcement (8 minutes left for group work)
6	4	Two students sharing a book; one student trying to borrow colored pencils for the crest (Capulet); one student reading teacher handout	Teacher now walking around the room, moving from Group 1 to Group 2 ... Teacher announces 4 minutes left ... asks for a volunteer group to share artistic rendition of the family/royal crest ... teacher moves to the front of the room to set up the overhead projector, and CD player ... teacher moves back to Group 5 ... asks for examples of foreshadowing ... calls time by asking the question: "How does Shakespeare use foreshadowing from scene 2 forward? ... students start to move desks around to break out of groups

Suggested Postobservation Conference Strategies

♦ Ask the teacher look for her patterns monitoring and moving from group to group.

ALTERNATIVE APPROACH TO COLLECTING DATA RELATED TO COOPERATIVE LEARNING

Tool 31: Tracking Teacher Behaviors Promoting Cooperative Learning

Teacher: **Janie Adams**   Date of Observation: **April 25, 2008**

Observer: **Brenda Arlin**

Class: **U.S. History**   Period of the Day: **2nd period**

Time of Observation: Start: **9:05**   End: **9:25**

Total Time Spent in Observation: **20 minutes**

Number of Students Present: **26**   Grade Level: **Juniors**

Topic of the Lesson: **Examining how a bill is passed**

Date of Postobservation Conference: **April 28, 2008**

Focus on Cooperative Learning	Presence or Absence	Notes
Objectives for the cooperative learning group	X	✓ Objective for the activity was written on the whiteboard ✓ Teacher referred to the objective as students asked questions. ✓ Teacher returned to the objective during closure of group activity.
Clarity of directions	X	✓ Before breaking students into groups, teacher gave directions. ✓ Teacher distributed directions for each group once students moved into their groups.
Movement into groups	X	✓ Six minutes were given for students to move into groups. ✓ Materials were bundled for each group in advance of movement.

Tool continues on next page.

Focus on Cooperative Learning	Presence or Absence	Notes
Monitoring and intervening strategies	X	✓ Teacher turned lights on and off to get attention. ✓ Teacher broke into group time three times with clarifying directions. ✓ Teacher visited each group four times.
Evaluation Strategies		
Interaction with students	X	✓ Teacher asked questions and gave feedback to groups while monitoring. ✓ Teacher clarified directions. ✓ Teacher became a member of each group.
Follow-up instruction— large-group processing	X	✓ After 19 minutes, teacher called end to group work. ✓ Students moved desks and chairs back in order. ✓ Group reporter gave report. ✓ Teacher asked and answered questions.

Suggested Postobservation Conference Strategies

Ask the teacher to review patterns associated with giving directions and clarifying information, the amount of time to get into cooperative groups, and movement from group-to-group.

TECHNOLOGY IMPLEMENTATION AND INTEGRATION

Background

Technology in the form of computers and peripheral components has been in place in our schools since the 1970s. Technology can bring the outside world into a classroom. Advances in technology and its availability have changed the way many teachers forward instruction and support student learning. Technology can be used to differentiate instruction, particularly in small-group or individualized instruction. Used in classroom activities, technology can be used to explore our universe, provide instructional support through games, reviews, simulations, and tutorials—all to extend learning opportunities by enhancing critical thinking and problem-solving skills.

However, just having access to computers and software in a classroom does not ensure technology integration. Teachers need to purposefully plan for technology integration, and principals can provide feedback on these efforts and extend discussions with teachers who are attempting to integrate technology with their teaching. According to a report of the Northwest Regional Educational Laboratory (NREL) (n.d.), the following list, although not exhaustive, shows a range of ways in which technology can be integrated:

- using integrated learning system in a subject;
- allowing, encouraging, or requiring students to use word processing and presentation software in reports and displays;
- requiring papers to be done on a word processor;
- using presentation software and projection technology for teacher presentations; and
- using computers for online testing and analysis of test results (p. 1).

NREL asserts that technology integration is occurring if:

- teachers are trained in a full range of technology uses and in the determination of their appropriate roles and applications;
- teachers and students routinely turn to technology when needed; and
- teachers and students are empowered and supported in carrying out those choices (p. 2).

Finally, NREL offers that there are certain actions and characteristics that teachers exhibit to promote technology integration. These actions and characteristics not only occur in the classroom but are also apparent in the planning and design of lessons and interactions among teachers.

- Teachers use technology in several ways, and such use is observable daily.
- Teachers routinely choose the technologies appropriate to their activity and need.
- Teachers are using online access to information resources from within the school and from home or other outside settings.
- Promising or successful practices are often shared between and among teachers.
- Teachers participate in the process of developing the guidelines for technology standards in curriculum areas.
- Teachers follow the guidelines for technology use in the curriculum.
- Teachers involve students in identifying a range of ways technology may be used to accomplish curricular objectives.

- Teachers expect and encourage independence of students in choosing and using technologies appropriate to their tasks.
- Teachers design assignments for students based on assumptions of technology use (p. 5).

Observation focus: How technology is integrated within teaching.

Observation technique: Mixed methods of data collection are used including a checklist and running anecdotal notes throughout the classroom observation.

Explanation of the tool and the technique: Data are collected using a mixed-method approach detailed in *The Classroom Observation Guide to Track Technology Integration** (Tool 32).

How and why the technique is helpful: This tool allows the principal to observe for a variety of ways in which technology is being integrated throughout instruction and the ways in which students are engaging in technological applications. The tool is also flexible enough to support recording open-ended notes to chronicle the uses of technology.

Directions and approaches for using the tool: Script notes as events in the classroom unfold. Check off items in the *Classroom Observation Guide to Track Technology Integration* (Tool 32) related to technology integration within the structure of the lesson being observed.

Tips

- Take detailed scripted notes and use the scripted notes to extend discussion.
- Note not only how technology is being integrated by the instructor but also note how students are using technology, either in groups or independently.

**The Classroom Observation Guide to Track Technology Integration Tool* was developed by Ann G. Haughey as part of her coursework in supervision theory and her problem of practice while working toward her specialist in education degree at the University of Georgia. Ann G. Haughey is the technology coordinator for Wilkes County Schools (Washington, GA).

Tool 32: Classroom Observation Guide to Track Technology Integration

Teacher's Name: **Art Roberson**   Observation Date: **September 8, 2008**

Observer: **Cindy Fields**

Class: **Social Studies**   Period of the Day: **Morning Block**

Time of Observation: Start: **10:10**   End: **10:30**

Total Time Spent in Observation: **20 Minutes**

Number of Students Present: **17**   Grade Level: **7th**

Topic of Lesson: **Immigrants and Ellis Island**

Date of Postobservation Conference: **September 9, 2008**

Indicators for Technology Integration

Rate each of the following using this rating scale:

1 = *Little* evidence of technology use.

2 = *Some* evidence that technology is used in limited amounts and with simple tasks—more productivity oriented.

3 = Evidence that teacher *uses* technology and provides assistance to students with spreadsheets, word processing, demonstrations.

4 = Teacher is *comfortable* with technology use. A *variety* of technology is used daily, and technology is an integral part of classroom instruction.

5 = Not applicable to the lesson.

———————————

5 1. **Students use computers for drill and practice activities; use of stand-alone computer software.**

♦ Use of networkable programs such as Accelerated Reader and Accelerated Math

♦ Use of instructional Web-based software such as Riverdeep

4 2. **Students use computers for instructional purposes.**

♦ Use of computers for performance assessments—such as, PowerPoint, Excel, and so forth

♦ Use of computers for Web-based research using computers to gather data

♦ Using a combination of software and Web-based research to analyze data and draw conclusions

♦ Taking data and conclusions and presenting it using some type of multimedia presentation

4 3. Teacher uses presentation software such as PowerPoint during instruction.

4 4. Teacher uses projection tools during instruction.
  ♦ Uses overhead projector
  ♦ Uses multimedia projector
  ♦ Uses multimedia projector with VCR
  ♦ Uses multimedia projector with SmartBoard or ActivBoard

5 5. Teacher incorporates the use of other devices during instruction.
  ♦ Digital camera
  ♦ Scanner
  ♦ iPod
  ♦ Graphing calculators

4 6. Teacher incorporates technology within the lesson, and student work is indicative of seamless transitions between traditional instruction and technology integration.

Classroom Observation Running Notes

10:10–10:15: *Mr. Roberson spent approximately 5 minutes recapping information from the prior day: What occurred once immigrants arrived at Ellis Island (docking, medical exams), the large numbers of immigrants that arrived at Ellis Island between 1892 and 1924 (about 22 million), etc.*

10:10–10:15: *Pulls up a PowerPoint presentation that has several Web addresses for students to mark in their browsers, and he directs student pairs to go to the computers in the back of the room. Students already know their "pairs" and proceed to the back of the room. Computers are already "booted up." Directs students to type the URL http://teacher.scholastic.com/activities/immigration/tour/index .htm and then to wait for further directions. Roberson ensures students have the URL plugged in and are on the virtual tour of Ellis Island home page.*

10:10–10:18: *Directs pairs to begin the tour with the audio off and to click on each tour page (approximately seven "click points"). At the end of the tour, students are asked to click onto the immigration home page URL. Students are directed to read and review Yesterday and Today. Students are reading and reviewing these pages.*

10:10–10:23: Mr. Roberson asks students to return to their seats. Explains the next project: In pairs, "come up with three questions you have about the Ellis Island experience, and write these questions on a sheet of paper."

10:10–10:28: Calls time. Asks a person from each pair to share their questions. Mr. Roberson is at the front of the room, typing in the questions of each group. Develops a "master list" of questions.

10:10–10:30: Asks pairs to go to the computers and begin a Google search to try to find answers to their questions. Students return to their computers with notebooks and begin searching the Web for resources to answer their questions.

10:10–10:30: Observation ends.

Suggested Postobservation Conference Strategies

♦ Focus more on the scripted notes seeking clarification on how technology and its integration is supporting the curriculum and extending student learning.

♦ Focus attention on next steps of how what was experienced by students will be extended to other learning opportunities in upcoming class sessions.

♦ Seek clarification of how technology and its integration is supporting the curriculum and extending student learning.

♦ Focus attention on how the teacher will extend what was experienced by students to other learning opportunities in upcoming class sessions

♦ Here are some questions to help guide the discussion:

1. In the end, what will students do with the answers to their questions? Will they share the information with one another? If so, will students use technology, such as developing a PowerPoint presentation? Share Web sources?

2. What is the next step in this lesson?

WIDE ANGLE: NO FOCUS

Background

Some teachers might want to get a general idea of how things are going in the classroom. The wide-angle lens enables the principal to observe, generally, what is occurring in the classroom.

Observation focus: Open-ended, no focus.

Observation technique: Anecdotal notes are taken as instruction and classroom activities unfold.

Explanation of the tool and technique: The observer writes down as much information as possible, chronicling the activities, instructional methods in use, transition strategies, words of the teacher or of the students, and any other details to provide a broad view of what was observed.

How and why the technique is helpful: Sometimes teachers just want to know generally what was occurring during specific periods of instruction.

Directions and approaches for using the tool: Indicate time and then chronicle what was occurring during the specified time. It is helpful to take notes in 5-minute chunks so that the teacher can see patterns during the time in which the notes were taken.

Tips

- Record events in 5-minute intervals.
- Record enough information so that the teacher can make sense of the overall events of the classroom.
- Include verbal statements as necessary to focus conversation during follow-up with the teacher.
- Avoid making value judgments while chronicling what is observed.

Tool 33:   Running Notes With a Timeline

Teacher: **Ron Kupinski**   Date of Observation: **April 28, 2008**

Observer: **Jesse Cantu**

Class: **5th Grade**   Period of the Day: **Morning**

Time of Observation: Start: **10:00**   End: **10:21**

Total Time Spent in Observation: **21 minutes**

Number of Students Present: **16**   Grade Level: **5th Grade**

Topic of the Lesson: **Fractions**

Date of Postobservation Conference: **April 29, 2008**

Time	Running Notes
10:05	✓ Students worked on a problem with the teacher leading students in a quick review of fractions and decimals in everyday situations (e.g., calculating sales tax). ✓ Had students work on a sample problem.
10:10	✓ Students worked at their desks—the students who needed additional help put their notebooks on the floor—this is the cue for Mr. Kupinski to go to their desk (about five students clustered in the back put their notebooks on the floor within 1 minute of starting the sample problem.
10:14	✓ Mr. Kupinski reviewed skills (adding fractions—like denominators and unlike denominators) ✓ Showed students how to add two mixed numbers whose fractions have the same denominator (used an overhead and then showed some computer-generated slides on a PowerPoint) ✓ Teacher: "Franklin, where is your head at today? Can't you figure this out? [Franklin stops talking but slams pencil down ... teacher stops teaching and writes in a notebook].
10:19	✓ Provided practice with students working adding two mixed numbers whose fractions have the same denominator

Suggested Postobservation Conference Strategies

To encourage reflection, consider open-ended questions such as:

♦ What do you think students learned during this time in the lesson?

♦ What will you do to follow up tomorrow?

♦ How can you assess what students were learning?

Looking Ahead ...

Now that an informal classroom observation has been conducted, what next? The next step is to be opportunistic and to find time to engage teachers in follow-up conversations. The intent is to foster discussion, reflection, and the momentum to refine practice.

5
Talking With Teachers After Looking In

In This Chapter ...

♦ Following up after an informal observation

♦ Postobservation conferences

♦ Lesson reconstruction

♦ Effective principals are prepared

♦ Approaches to the postobservation conference

♦ Feedback

♦ Next steps

You have accomplished quite a bit so far, but conducting informal classroom observations is not enough. The process is not complete without some type of follow-up discussion to the classroom observation, and this time-consuming meeting is why it is important for the principal to develop a manageable schedule of informal classroom observations. It is better to conduct fewer observations each week that include following up with the teacher than to conduct numerous observations without follow-up discussions. This chapter explores the follow-up process, feedback, and reflection with tips about the next steps that principals can take to enhance their efforts.

FOLLOWING UP AFTER AN INFORMAL OBSERVATION

To develop professionally, teachers need opportunities to talk, inquire, and reflect about their practices with the assistance of a colleague. A 20-minute informal observation yields fertile data, and the follow-up process adds value to the observation just conducted. The principal demonstrates respect for the work teachers do when immediate feedback is provided—both written and, perhaps more profound, through a purposeful discussion in which the meanings of data are explored, with the teacher assuming an active role in the process.

Worst-case scenarios include the principal who leaves a note in the teacher's mailbox without any follow-up discussion, no feedback at all, or written or oral feedback that is negative in nature. The informal observation method that this book promotes includes follow-up discussion but does not preclude written feedback as well. Really, a combination of oral and written feedback is essential to promote ongoing dialogue between the teacher and principal. Tool 34 details a written feedback form that is helpful to use as a prompt for follow-up discussion. Effective principals balance written and oral feedback. Some principals find it helpful to give written feedback immediately after the observation and then to follow up with discussion. By giving written feedback prior to the follow-up discussion, the teacher has time to absorb the information. However, some principals may find it useful to bring the written feedback to the postobservation conference. Time and circumstances will dictate which approach the principal takes.

Tool 34:   Sample Informal Postobservation Feedback Form

Teacher: **Patty Braveman**   Date of Observation: **May 22, 2008**

Observer: **Jennifer Spinks**

Class: **Spanish I**   Period of the Day: **2nd period**

Time of Observation: Start: **9:30**   End: **9:50**

Total Time Spent in Observation: **20 minutes**

Number of Students Present: **18**   Grade Level: **Mixed 9th, 10th, and 11th**

Topic of the Lesson: **How to tell time in Spanish**

Date of Postobservation Conference: **May 23, 2008**

Students were

- ☒ working in small, cooperative groups
- ☐ making a presentation
- ☐ taking a test
- ☒ working independently at their desks
- ☐ viewing a film
- ☐ other: Pair-share groups to practice telling time in Spanish

Teacher was

- ☒ lecturing
- ☐ facilitating a question and answer sequence
- ☐ working independently with students
- ☒ demonstrating a concept
- ☒ introducing a new concept
- ☐ reviewing for a test
- ☐ coming to closure
- ☐ other

Comments:

Patty: Wow and more Wow on your efforts to provide solid instruction and to engage a group of students in the lesson on how to tell time in Spanish. The introduction hooked students because you: (1) used prompts (e.g., the big clock, smaller clocks for each student and their groups), (2) incorporated the use of time with prior lesson content (e.g., ordering a meal, asking for directions, making a long-distance call in a different time zone, and (3) kept the small pair-share groups focused with written directions on the oral exercise to practice before getting back into large group.

Students were eager to share once the "round-robin time talk" began after your introductory lecture and the pair-share groups finished. The hands that flew up signaled that students were eager to show you what they had learned.

For our discussion later today, I am interested in how you gauge wait time in teaching a foreign language.

I look forward to our meeting.

—Jennifer Spinks

POSTOBSERVATION CONFERENCES

The intent of the postobservation conference is for the teacher and principal to

♦ review and analyze the data collected;

♦ reflect on meanings; and

♦ examine future possibilities for ongoing professional development and refinement of practice.

First and foremost, effective postobservation conferences are

♦ time bound;

♦ place bound; and

♦ dialogue bound.

Postobservation Conferences Are Time Bound

Time is important; if too much time elapses between the observation and the conference, the data lose meaning, and teachers lose motivation to learn from the process. Timely feedback occurs within 48 hours of the observation. Some principals meet with teachers immediately after the observation. To do this, the principal must plan a follow-up conversation with the teacher during a preparation period, meet with the teacher over lunch, or find a substitute for a portion of the teacher's duty period to facilitate conversation. As a principal, you are encouraged to become opportunistic and creative in finding time during the day to meet with teachers. Find time before, during, and after the day for follow-up opportunities.

Postobservation Conferences Are Place Bound

The place where follow-up occurs is significant. Holding the postobservation conference in the principal's office puts the principal in a position of authority. Conducting the postobservation conference in the classroom where the observation occurred helps to recreate the context of the learning environment. It also offers the teacher and principal appropriate and immediate props to demonstrate the points made in observation. Atmosphere is essential; the postobservation conference opens the door to future dialogue and growth. However, the library, media center, faculty lounge, and other accessible areas of the school provide appropriate places for the principal and teacher to meet. Although privacy is essential, public places should not be avoided. The principal who is out and about is visible talking with teachers between classes, during duty periods, at the bus stop, at sporting events—any place where teachers are.

Postobservation Conferences Are Dialogue Bound

McGreal (1983) asserted that the more teachers talk about teaching, the better they get at it. Postobservation conferences should invite ongoing dialogue between the teacher and principal. Although written follow-up is acceptable, effort should be made to engage teachers in discussion and reflection. Not only do teachers have an opportunity to talk about their teaching and analyze data during follow-up, but they also have the opportunity to

- ◆ reflect on practice;
- ◆ express concerns; and
- ◆ pinpoint areas they want to pursue further with formal and informal professional development

LESSON RECONSTRUCTION

One method, *lesson reconstruction* (Bellon & Bellon, 1982), elevates the teacher as an integral part of the active learning process, engaged as a learner in the process of deriving meaning from the analysis of data collected during classroom observation. The lesson-reconstruction method calls for follow up the same day, if possible. In this method, the teacher and the principal use the data to reconstruct the events of the classroom. The data drives the discussion, and the data helps the teacher reconstruct the lesson. One strategy to assist with lesson reconstruction is to leave the notes from the observation with the teacher while exiting the classroom (see Tool 35). Included with the raw observation notes should be the time and place of the postobservation conference to ensure that this important aspect of the informal observation does not get put on the "back burner" because of distraction caused by other responsibilities.

Tool 35:   Presentation of Postobservation Conference Notes

Teacher: **Ron Kupinski**   Date of Observation: **April 28, 2008**

Observer: **Jesse Cantu**

Class: **Grade 5**   Period of the Day: **Morning**

Time of Observation: Start: **10:00**   End: **10:21**

Total Time Spent in Observation: **21 minutes**

Number of Students Present: **16**   Grade Level: **5th grade**

Topic of the Lesson: **Fractions, Decimals, and Integers**

Date of Postobservation Conference: **April 29, 2008—3rd Period [Ron, I have a sub for your assigned duty period. Let's meet in your classroom, Jesse.]**

Time	Running Notes	Teacher Questions
10:05	✓ Students worked on a problem with the teacher leading students in a quick review of fractions and decimals in every day situations (tax).	Was my review too brisk given the observation that five students needed help within 1 minute of starting independent practice?
10:10	✓ Had students work on a sample problem. ✓ Students worked at their desks—the students who needed additional help put their notebooks on the floor floor—this is the cue for Mr. Kupinski to go to their desk (about five students clustered in the back put their notebooks on the floor within 1 minute of starting the sample problem.	

Tool continues on next page.

Time	Running Notes	Teacher Questions
10:14	✓ Showed students to add two mixed numbers whose fractions have the same denominator (used an overhead and then showed some computer-generated slides on a PowerPoint presentation). ✓ Teacher: "Franklin, where is your head at today? Can't you figure this out? [Franklin stops talking but slams pencil down ... teacher stops teaching and writes in a notebook.]	I can't get a sense of how often to review—I think they get it and then, wham, I lose two or three students. I'm thinking about appealing more to multiple intelligences ... but I use overheads and other technology. Any ideas? I need help with Franklin—today he was mild.
10:19	✓ Provided practice with students working on problems related to adding mixed numbers.	

If the principal leaves these notes with the teacher, the teacher will need to take time to reflect on the data and pose questions based on the observation notes. During the follow-up discussion, the teacher and principal review the notes and the corresponding questions the teacher has written on the form. From there, the teacher and principal engage in a discussion of the data. Although spontaneity is encouraged, the events chronicled by the principal frame the discussion. The following questions are useful in guiding the discussion:

- How do you think the lesson went?
- What went well?
- What would you do again if you were teaching this same lesson?
- What would you do differently?
- Overall, how do you think this lesson went in comparison to the same lesson taught with a different group of students?

Again, the data and the teacher's insights will frame the discussion. This technique points to the importance of the principal's ability to chronicle data during the classroom observation.

EFFECTIVE PRINCIPALS ARE PREPARED

Being prepared for discussion during follow-up with the teacher is essential; principals make judgment calls on whether follow-up should be done in writing, orally, or a combination of both. Planning time gives the principal the opportunity to organize the raw data gathered during the observation. Teaching is fast paced, and the principal records observations at an equally fast pace. In its final form, the data must be clear and understandable to both the teacher and the principal. To lay the groundwork for a successful postobservation conference, the principal tackles several tasks:

♦ *Revisit the focus of the classroom observation.* Within the first minute or so of the informal classroom observation, the principal makes a major decision—what he or she will focus on during the length of the classroom observation. This focus determines the type of data collection method and tool that will be used to chronicle the events of the classroom observation. Reviewing the data, the principal looks for direct or striking examples of classroom practices that relate specifically to the focus. One approach is to identify events that either contributed to or prevented the teacher from achieving an objective.

♦ *Develop a strategy for presenting the data collected during the observation.* Providing the teacher with objective feedback is dependent on displaying the data clearly and the ability to return to the data for clarification, explanation, or extension during the postobservation conference. The observer's role is to facilitate the teacher's reflection and self-analysis by way of the data. The conference plan should keep the teacher reflecting on and analyzing the events of the classroom.

♦ *Frame an opening to get the teacher thinking and talking about teaching.* Effective invitations to dialogue, also called "icebreakers," are open-ended statements related to some aspect of teaching. The intent of an icebreaker statement is to get the teacher talking about events of the classroom. Conversely, conversation-stopper statement put open-ended discussions on ice. Conversation-stoppers create a chill, thwarting open-ended discussions. Figure 5.1 presents examples of icebreaker and conversation-stopper statements.

APPROACHES TO THE POSTOBSERVATION CONFERENCE

To make the follow-up discussion more inviting and meaningful, a facilitative style, in which the principal is open to hearing what the teacher has to say, will be most helpful to the teacher. Remember, the follow-up discussion is about the teacher, not the principal. The teacher's point of view must permeate the discussion. Talking about teaching is a cooperative endeavor. It is the principal's duty to engage the teacher in reviewing, analyzing, and reflecting on data. Through effort, patience,

Figure 5.1. Comparison of Postobservation Icebreaker and Conversation-Stopper Statements

Icebreaker Statements	Conversation Stoppers
◆ Think back to [some aspect of the lesson or the class] and tell me about it.	◆ Prove to me that the students were prepared for independent practice.
◆ The approach you chose to break students into small groups helped students learn how to cooperate. Tell me how you were able to get students to this level of cooperation.	◆ Do you think it's wise to allow your at-risk student the freedom that cooperative groups encourage?
◆ Tell me more about _____.	◆ Don't you think that more guided practice would have been more appropriate?
◆ When you looked at Johnny, he knew immediately to stop talking. How did you know how and when to look at him like this? Is Johnny the only student who responds to your look to stop talking? How did you know to use that look?	◆ Don't get too confident about Johnny, he'll talk while you are working with other students
◆ For the students who were absent the day before, you used activity time to help them catch up. What about the students in the activity? Can the students catch up another way?	◆ Just analyze my notes and then get back to me if you have any questions about my assessment of your teaching.
◆ How did you know that the student would try to …	◆ Stop babying these kids; they are about to graduate and need to be more self-sufficient, don't you agree?

and willingness to be of assistance, principals can help teachers make progress in their professional development. To establish a collaborative relationship with the teacher, the supervisor's style and approach to communication must promote teacher talk. Figure 5.2 identifies ways to promote teacher dialogue, inquiry, and reflection.

Figure 5.2. Approaches to Promoting Dialogue, Inquiry, and Reflection

Approach	*Example*
♦ Remain objective by providing the teacher with observational data that is value-free and nonjudgmental. ♦ Listen more—talk less—in order to hear (understand) what the teacher is trying to communicate.	♦ Here are the events that led to the small group…
♦ Acknowledge, paraphrase, and ask probing and clarifying questions that encourage the teacher to talk more. ♦ Open-ended questions help the teacher make discoveries, identify recurring patterns, and reflect on possible alternatives or extensions to instructional practices. ♦ Encourage the teacher to expand on statements that share beliefs about teaching, learning, and students.	♦ Examine the following notes and tell me what responses you anticipated from students after you asked for … ♦ From your point of view, what made this lesson successful? At what point did you sense the students were "getting it"?
♦ State what went well and ask reflective questions to focus on what needs improvement from the teacher's point of view. ♦ Avoid giving directive types of advice—even if asked. Instead engage the teacher in role-playing reprises of events you observed, then invite extended thinking. Role-playing and simulations that reflect the teacher's practices are more realistic.	♦ When the student in the red shirt said, "This is stupid," what made it possible for you to continue with activity. ♦ The small group activity really worked well. How do you think the transition back to large group could have been different. ♦ Let me pretend I am a student in your fourth hour class. How would you help me understand the concepts important to today's unit discussion
♦ Refuse to engage in talk not related to what you directly observed or to the improvement of instruction.	♦ That thought is important. After the postobservation conference, I'll share your idea with the assistant principal.
♦ Offer to return for further observations in order to keep the momentum going for the teacher.	♦ When would be a good time for me to come back to see the students apply the formula?

Figure continues on next page.

◆ Provide ongoing support for the decisions the teacher makes in the postobservation conference by investigating with the teacher follow-up learning or enrichment activities.	◆ The district is offering an after-school workshop on higher order thinking. Perhaps you'd like to go. Would you like me to make a reservation for you?
◆ Be aware of nonverbal behavior that can send mixed messages. Convey interest and concern.	◆ Looking at the clock, facial expressions, and body language such as folded arms.

FEEDBACK

Teachers need and want to know how they are doing and what they can do to improve or modify an approach; moreover, teachers need to be affirmed for their efforts. Data should be the only source of feedback, and the principal should take care not to impose bias or judgment on observation data. Framing and giving feedback are complicated. People want praise for their efforts, but they also want honesty when their efforts need adjustment. It is often easier to give positive rather than negative feedback. Providing both types of feedback will require tact, wise word choice, and clear communication. Principals cannot afford any hidden messages in their words. Hidden messages can enhance or block the future efforts of the principal and teacher.

Types of Feedback

Feedback can be confirmatory or corrective, according to Kurtoglu-Hooton (2004) who details the work of Egan (2002). Based on the preliminary research of Kurtoglu-Hooton (pp. 1–3), confirmatory feedback is given in the context of praise in connection with what the teacher did well and is likely to encourage a teacher to construct his/her own constructive thought patterns and may encourage teachers to try new avenues and to pursue new challenges.

Conversely, corrective feedback is

◆ based on expected behaviors

◆ applied to situations where there may have been a better course of action

◆ "a gentle telling off" if the teacher seems to be repeating the same mistakes without any evidence of moving forward. Corrective feedback requires a period of time for the teacher to process, digest, reflect upon and come to terms with the "criticism" involved.

Kurtoglu-Hooton (2004) also asserted that confirmatory feedback is often less detailed than corrective feedback.

Feedback can be constructive or destructive. Consider the following statements:

1. "Mrs. Ritter, you really need to take the workshop. All the questions you asked were lower-level ones. Students were obviously bored with your class."

2. "Mrs. Ritter, your insight about your questions asking students for recall reminds me of how I used to ask opening questions. I benefited from the county workshop *Questioning Strategies That Promote Higher-Order Thinking.* This session is on the schedule for next month; would you be interested in attending? We have the funds and with advance notice, I can lock in a sub for you."

Statement 1 is destructive; it is too blunt, and it puts the teacher down with a personal attack. Statement 2 communicates the same message—the teacher needs assistance with questioning strategies—but in a more productive way.

Constructive feedback provides objective insight based on data without criticizing the teacher or finding fault. This type of feedback promotes a willingness to take risks and to be more open to changing practice. Destructive feedback, by contrast, belittles teachers by compiling data that point only to weaknesses or attacks aspects of instruction that are beyond the teacher's control. Figure 5.3 lists characteristics of effective feedback.

DATA OVERLOAD

In an attempt to be helpful, some principals fall into the trap of overwhelming the teacher with too much information. Principals who attempt to establish their credibility may fall into the trap of offering a laundry list of observations based on their view of the lesson. But supervision is not about the principal; supervision is about the teacher and the learning opportunity that the data and feedback from an observation can provide. The tenor of the feed-back in the postobservation conference sets the tone for future interaction between the principal and the teacher.

Of course, even carefully framed feedback may not be well received. The way a teacher receives feedback depends on variables such as the degree of trust between the supervisor and teacher, the experience level of the teacher, the patterns of communication at the school, and the conditions surrounding the classroom observation.

Feedback is effective because of its frequency, timing, specificity, and contextualized nature.

♦ *Frequency:* Feedback should be given often (this means that principals need to get supervision "out of the main office").

Figure 5.3. Characteristics of Effective Feedback

Effective feedback in the postobservation conference does the following:

♦ Supports the teacher in examining both the positive and the not-so-positive aspects of practice;

♦ Creates footholds for follow-up;

♦ Nurtures a sense of worth and positive self-esteem;

♦ Facilitates self-assessment and self-discovery;

♦ Focuses on a few key areas;

♦ Describes accurately what was observed;

♦ Is authentic and free of meaningless or patronizing platitudes;

♦ Clarifies and expands ideas for both the teacher and the observer

♦ Deals with concrete, observed examples;

♦ Promotes goal setting and the development of strategies;

♦ Guides the teacher in thinking beyond the lesson observed; and

♦ Acknowledges and incorporates the points the teacher makes as part of the feedback process.

Effective feedback avoids:

♦ Making assumptions about teachers;

♦ Overloading the teacher with detail after detail after detail;

♦ Offering global generalizations about the teacher's credibility; and

♦ Judging and labeling a practice as good or bad.

♦ *Timing:* Feedback should be given as soon as humanly possible after a formal or informal observation. Time fades the memory. Think of the difficulties in recreating the events of the classroom even with stable data collected during an observation.

♦ *Specificity:* With stable data, feedback should be related to specific events as they unfolded in the classroom.

♦ *Contextualized nature:* Feedback must take into consideration classroom variables such as the characteristics of students, the experience level of the teacher, and the focus of the classroom observation.

Feedback is critical to any instructional supervisory model. Without feedback after a classroom observation, it is unlikely that growth and development will occur or that teachers will make changes in their classroom practices.

NEXT STEPS

The follow-up process extends beyond the feedback and links informal classroom observations to professional development. Through a series of informal classroom observations with written and verbal feedback, both the teacher and the principal are aware of areas to focus in the future. Informal classroom observations and the discussions during postobservation conferences provide windows of opportunities to connect that work with professional development. Through the purposeful interactions, the principal discovers

- skills teachers are implementing in practice;
- skills that teachers are struggling to implement;
- what is working in practice—how, why, or why not;
- the ongoing support and resources that teachers need;
- follow-up activities needed to support implementation; and
- teachers who would be willing to let others observe their teaching.

To promote professional development, the teacher and principal should consider the following activities:

- attendance at workshops, seminars, and conferences;
- observation of another teacher in the building or district;
- enrollment in a graduate course;
- engagement in action research with a common grade or subject area teacher;
- formation of a study group after identifying a topic of interest; and
- development or refinement of a portfolio.

The principal, who seeks to learn what a teacher needs to reach the next level of performance, remembers to follow through with support. With a hectic day, a large faculty, multiple tasks not related to instruction, and competing interests to focus attention, a simple "tracking sheet" can help jog the principal's memory of teacher's interests and short and long-term goals. A principal in the field keeps a notebook in which she logs the needs of her teachers based on what she observes in classrooms and the conversations she has with them after the observation. Although it takes a couple of minutes to update after every formal and informal classroom observation, this type of tracking adds credibility in that teachers know she will follow-through with information, opportunities, and discussions in between classroom observations. Tool 36 is a sample of what a tracking sheet might look like.

Tool 36: Tracking Sheet—Faculty Needs

Teacher: *Jillian Clarke*   Years: 2008 to _____

Years at Mercer High School =   *12 [biology and life science]*

Short-Term Instructional Goal(s):   *(1) learn more about cooperative learning related to labs*

Long-Term Instructional Goal(s):   *(1) complete doctorate*
(2) National Board Certification

Log of Informal Observations

Observation Date: 09/12/08
Follow-up:
- **check on system offerings for cooperative learning (spring and summer)**
- **pull article, "101 Reasons for Using Cooperative Learning in Biology Teaching" (Thomas R. Lord)**
- **start subscription for The American Biology Teacher; ask the Learning Media Center director to e-mail Jillian when the issues start arriving**

Observation Date: 10/10/08
Follow-up:
- **check with district science coordinator about summer curriculum work and seminars available at Argonne National Laboratory**
- **check calendar for next week—Jillian requested that I do an informal observation during 6th hour on either a Monday or a Thursday to observe a lab—focus on classroom traffic and monitoring lab pairings—get seating chart**
- **note sent to custodians to get power strips in 312 and 313 (lab)**
- **check to see if Ms. Nesbitt would want to observe Jillian teach**

Tips

- Keep the tracking sheet simple;
- Put aside 10 minutes a day to update information based on the day's informal observations (even formal observations);
- Encourage other administrators to keep a similar type of notebook; and
- Use a three-ring notebook and keep adding sheets for each teacher so to have a running history that spans the teacher's career.

The possibilities are endless. Follow-up holds great promise as a supervisory tool. During this time, teachers have the opportunity to analyze and make sense of data that bring some aspect of their teaching into focus. Lesson reconstruction as advocated by Bellon and Bellon (1982) engages the teacher in rebuilding the events of the classroom using data to analyze effectiveness. When the principal offers objective feedback, the teacher is in a better position to make informed judgments about practice and to develop further plans for growth and change.

Looking Ahead ...

The power of any discussion about what occurred in a classroom can be enhanced by studying student work. Some techniques and tips about incorporating the examination of student work samples during a postobservation conference are explored in the next chapter.

6

Studying Student Work During and After Classroom Observations

In This Chapter ...

- ♦ Focusing on student learning
- ♦ How informal classroom observations can help teachers examine student work
- ♦ Getting started with examining student work

INTRODUCTION

While in a classroom, the principal should strive to keep "one eye on the teacher and the other eye on the students" a maxim I adopted only after years of conducting informal and formal classroom observations. Through time in the field, I marvel when principals, assistant principals, instructional coaches, and other support personnel come to realize that classroom observations are about studying how

- ♦ students react to instruction;
- ♦ students respond as they are learning "X" from their teachers or interactions with other students; and
- ♦ students, teachers, and content knowledge interact—this is learning!

Through purposeful observations, principals see first-hand student work and artifacts of learning. Principals often see these artifacts as they are being created live in the classroom. Principals observe students answering questions, writing problems across white boards (or blackboards), composing letters on computer screens, draw-

127

ing, singing, calculating, and a host of other activities in which artifacts of learning are embedded.

As a strategy to support teacher learning, the discussions during postobservation conferences can be enhanced through examining student work. Through collaborative discussions, the meanings embedded within student work artifacts can help:

1. teachers think about their teaching;
2. teachers learn more about their students; and
3. teachers and principals identify professional development opportunities.

Through the process of examining student work with teachers, the principal can stimulate reflection, support change in practices, and help teachers see squarely what students are or are not learning. The analysis of artifacts of teaching—student work—can yield powerful insights about teaching while providing equally powerful learning opportunities for teachers. Sounds like a win-win situation!

FOCUSING ON STUDENT WORK

As a strategy for teacher development, the informal classroom observation is job-embedded because the work of teaching, refining instructional practices, and meeting the needs of students coalesce into opportunities for teachers to see live the impact of efforts on student learning. Teaching and learning occurs in a context—the classroom. Examining student work leads teachers to learn more about the efforts of their teaching. Here are some fundamental questions to think about:

♦   What can the artifacts of teaching tell a teacher?
♦   How does a teacher make sense out of student work?
♦   How many artifacts does a teacher need to know whether or not learning is "sticking?"

These are interesting questions that do not have "pat answers." What is known with certainty is that "when teachers analyze and discuss instructional practice and the resulting samples of student work, they experience some of the highest caliber professional development available" (The National Educational Association Foundation for the Improvement of Education, 2003, p. 2).

Although informal observations are brief, much can be observed in 15 to 20 minutes. The real action occurs during the discussion after the observation. There is a great deal of complexity surrounding the examination of student work. In fact, examining student work is professional development that should be sustained over time among teachers and others (Zepeda, 2008). However, there is room at the table for principals to engage teachers in discussions about student work and artifacts of learning as follow-up to informal and formal classroom observations. The study of student work can include many artifacts such as essays, art work, science experiments, blueprints, and so forth. The study of student work is a critical source of information about learning and teaching. Astute principals purposefully seek out this type of learning opportunities for their teachers.

How Informal Classroom Observations Can Help Teachers Examine Student Work

Although most teachers can identify the gaps in their own teaching and student understanding, principals can play a pivotal role in helping teachers to examine student work samples. Principals can help teachers make sense of student artifacts if they have collected stable data about instructional practices during informal observations. Let's look at a scenario here, reflecting on the following data from an informal classroom observation (Figure 6.1).

Suggested Postobservation Conference Strategies

Later the same day, Julie Escobar visited Shelly Beter for a few minutes and asked her to review the observation notes so she could analyze the data on her own. The next day, Julie and Shelly met before school to discuss the classroom observation. Julie began the conversation with an open-ended question, "What patterns do you see in the data?"

During the postobservation conference, Julie and Shelly reviewed the various instructional strategies used, the amount of time spent on each, what students were doing during each, and what learning objectives were being met. On reflection, Shelly shared that she really did not give students enough time to write out ideas and concepts on the note cards and that she would experiment with (1) extending the amount of time for note taking and (2) giving more explicit directions to students prior to having them work independently. She shared that some students were still having difficulties with finding "proofs" from the text of the novel.

Go back to the classroom observation notes where Shelly asked her students to write one sentence about the importance of the Siamese fighting fish and then later she asks students to find citation proofs from the book to support their interpretation of the symbolism of the Siamese fighting fish. In the postobservation conference, Shelly comes to the conclusion after viewing the data that she did not give students enough time to write out their thoughts and that some students were still having difficulties with finding "proofs" from the text of the novel.

Although we know from the amount of time indicated in the observation notes that Shelly did not give students enough time to write their thoughts, we really do not know what the thoughts were and how students substantiated their thoughts with passages from the book, *Rumble Fish*.

Figure 6.1. Data From an Informal Classroom Observation

Teacher: **Shelly Beter** Date of Observation: **March 4, 2008**

Observer: **Julie Escobar**

Class: **English I (Remedial)** Period of the Day: **Block 1**

Time of Observation: Start: **9:00** End: **9:25**

Total Time Spent in Observation: **25 minutes**

Number of Students Present: **25** Grade Level: **9th grade**

Topic of the Lesson: **S. E. Hinton's Rumble Fish**

Date of Postobservation Conference: **March 4, 2008**

Time	Instructional Method	Teacher Behavior	Student Activities
9:00– 9:05	Organizing lecture	Lecturing, Q & A period about plot Distributes an index card to each student: Directs students to write one sentence about the importance of the Siamese fighting fish	Listening, taking notes, Asking questions
9:06– 9:08	Independent work	Monitoring student work	Students write on the index cards
9:09– 9:22	Large-group sharing	Teacher seeks volunteers to share insights about the Siamese fighting fish and its importance thus far in the book; asking for "proofs" from the text to support ideas written on the index cards Leading students to citations offered by groups	Sharing thoughts about the symbol of the Siamese fighting fish; finding citations from the text to support ideas
9:23– 9:25	Question and answer	Asking questions	Responding to questions (looking up citations to back up ideas); asking questions

Figure 6.2. Examining Student Work

Student Thought	Proofs from the Book
People are like animals	Rusty-James said, "The animals reminded me of people" (p. 13)
	In the end, the gangs are likened to "Siamese fighting fish." They "destroy one another."
	Motorcycle Boy breaks into the pet store.
	Motorcycle Boy heads for the river shortly after the break-in to the pet store.

Here is the principal's cue in this case for getting the artifacts of student work into the postobservation conference. Before the postobservation conference, Julie Escobar could ask Ms. Beter to bring the student note cards and the proofs they had written on the back of the note cards.

Figure 6.2 illustrates how examining the note cards with the student's thoughts about the book alongside the proofs could help Shelly dig deeper about what skills her students were learning and how she could perhaps adjust her instruction to re-teach how to use proofs to back up ideas found in this book.

Tool 37 can serve as a guide to examine student-generated artifacts (in this instance, the note cards and the proofs).

The objective is to look at the student work for indicators of what worked and what did not work in the lesson, but a more important priority is to encourage the teacher to look at ways to make mid-course changes in instruction. The value of timely postobservation conferences is that teachers can reflect more immediately on their practices and then make modifications if and as necessary. The principal serves as the mirror for the teacher to examine instructional practices. Through this effort, teachers can identify cues on what instructional practices or curricular materials need to be modified.

Examining student work can help teachers to make better decisions related to the curriculum and its development, instructional strategies, and assessments. It would be interesting to see what Ms. Beter would do today based on her reflections from the previous day and the discussion during the postobservation conference.

Tool 37: Questions to Lead the Teacher Talk About Student-Generated Artifacts

1. What information about student learning have you gleaned from the student thoughts and proofs from the cards?

2. Do the cards later get used so students can write an essay?

3. Today, what will you do to review the proofs and the cards with students?

4. What do these artifacts tell you about what you are teaching and why?

5. If you could rework the lesson from yesterday, what would you do differently and why?

6. How can this lesson and in-class assignment be modified based on the patterns found in these cards and the proofs?

Examining Artifacts can Help With Further Planning

It is unlikely that Ms. Julie Escobar will be able to visit Shelly Beter's class today, but the knowledge gained from examining artifacts can serve another purpose—planning for future instruction based on the decisions made by the teacher. Through examination of the artifacts and the other classroom observation notes, Ms. Beter is in a position to plan out with the live feedback from the principal, what instruction will look like for these students.

GETTING STARTED WITH EXAMINING STUDENT WORK

Getting started examining student work can be awkward for teachers because they are sharing their "vulnerabilities" in full view of another person. The principal reassures teachers that conversations about student work are all about learning about how to teach better, how better to develop curricular approaches, and how to modify instructional and curricular approaches based on what is learned while examining student work. A leader can assist teachers with getting started with the process of examining student work by providing time in postobservation conferences to examine student work.

What Work to Examine?

The National Education Association (2003) underscores that "data are more than test scores" (p. 1). Teachers, who are at the beginning stages of examining student work, can be assisted with agreeing on a single standard (curricular/learning) and then examine student work samples that reflect that standard. Work samples could include:

- essays;
- quiz or test sample responses;
- video-clips of students completing tasks; and
- drawings.

Any item that is a sample of student work can be studied. The objective is to study not only the artifact but also the learning objective, the standard, and the instructional approach to see how students perform, what have they mastered, what shifts in instructional practices need to be made.

How to Go About Studying Student Work

A primary objective behind studying student work is to "invite conversations about the work and the teaching associated with it" (McDonald, 2001, p. 121). However, McDonald offers that the conversations are "highly structured," employ some type of "protocol" and that "the activity of talking productively with peers about the intentions behind and the actual effects of one's work demands assertiveness and frankness but also requires delicacy and some buffer against quick judgments and harsh words" (p. 121).

McDonald believes "the discipline and structure make the process safe" (p. 122). The intent is to "suspend judgment" so "that the teacher finds her capacity to make judgments enriched by other perspectives" (McDonald, 2001, p. 122). ATLAS Learning Communities, Inc. (2007) offers sound strategies to get teachers reflecting, listening, and collaborating while studying student work. Although the examination of student work often occurs among groups of teachers, the principal and the teacher can make significant gains in understanding teaching, learning, and assessment by undertaking this work. Tool 38 presents a protocol that can be used in a postobservation conference by the teacher and principal to examine student work samples and artifacts. This tool is adapted from one developed by ATLAS Learning Communities, Inc.

Tool 38: Thinking, Listening and Reflecting With Colleagues About Student Work*

Reflecting on the process

Looking for evidence of student thinking ...

- ◆ What did you see in this student's work that was interesting or surprising?

- ◆ What did you learn about how this student thinks and learns?

- ◆ What about the process helped you to see and learn these things?

Reflecting on one's own thinking ...

- ◆ What questions about teaching and assessment did looking at the students' work raise for you?

- ◆ How can you pursue these questions further?

- ◆ Are there things you would like to try in your classroom as a result of looking at this student's work?

Source: *Copyright 2007 ATLAS Learning Communities. Adapted and used with permission.

Another way to frame the discussion of student work is to examine content standards and the adopted curriculum for the school system. Tool 39 provides a sample guide to help the principal frame the examination of student work around content standards adopted by the school system.

Tool 39: Examining Student Work by Content Standards

Teacher: **Shelly Beter**　　　　Date of Observation: **March 4, 2008**

Observer: **Julie Escobar**

Class: **English I (Remedial)**　　　Period of the Day: **Block 1**

Time of Observation: Start: **9:00**　　End: **9:25**

Total Time Spent in Observation: **25 minutes**

Number of Students Present: **25**　　　Grade Level: **9th grade**

Topic of the Lesson: **S. E. Hinton's Rumble Fish**

Date of Postobservation Conference: **March 4, 2008**

Artifact: One student essay. Essay assignment: Develop an essay of 950 words in which two symbols from *Rumble Fish* are used to foreshadow the ending of the book.
Standards Grade 9—English

Narrative Analysis of Grade-Level-Appropriate Text

3.3. Analyze interactions between main and subordinate characters in a literary text (e.g., internal and external conflicts, motivations, relationships, influences) and explain the way those interactions affect the plot.

3.7. Recognize and understand the significance of various literary devices, including figurative language, imagery, allegory, and symbolism, and explain their appeal.

Writing Strategies

1.1. Students write coherent and focused essays that convey a well-defined perspective and tightly reasoned argument. The writing demonstrates students' awareness of the audience and purpose. Students progress through the stages of the writing process as needed.

Organization and Focus

1.1. Establish a controlling impression or coherent thesis that conveys a clear and distinctive perspective on the subject and maintain a consistent tone and focus throughout the piece of writing.

1.2. Use precise language, action verbs, sensory details, appropriate modifiers, and the active rather than the passive voice.

Tool continues on next page.

> *Research and Technology*
>
> 1.4. Develop the main ideas within the body of the composition through supporting evidence (e.g., scenarios, commonly held beliefs, hypotheses, definitions).
>
> 1.6. Integrate quotations and citations into a written text while maintaining the flow of ideas.
>
> 1.7. Use appropriate conventions for documentation in the text, notes, and bibliographies by adhering to those in style manuals (e.g., *Modern Language Association Handbook, The Chicago Manual of Style*).
>
> 1.8. Design and publish documents by using advanced publishing software and graphic programs.
>
> **Questions to Guide the Examination and Discussion of the Student Essay:**
>
> 1. What were the objectives for the essay?
> 2. What content standards were being addresses:
> 3. What instruction was used prior to the students writing the essay?
>
> Based on this essay:
>
> 1. What examples from the essay illustrate the student has achieved the standard(s)?
> 2. What examples from the essay show there are gaps in mastery?
> 3. What types of instruction will be used to address these gaps? Or how will future instruction be modified?
> 4. What types of follow-up are provided for this student and others who do not meet the standards? Or for the students who meet or exceeds the standards?

The following tool (Tool 40) provides some prompts to help the principal and teacher "talk through" the planning of instruction based on the analysis of student work in the postobservation conference. The reader is encouraged to modify questions to fit the context of the work at the site.

Tool 40: Planning Guide—What Next?

1. What content needs to be reviewed or retaught based on the discussion during the postobservation conference?

2. What instructional strategies would most likely help move learning forward to meet goals and objectives?

3. What materials are needed?

As the principal and teacher gain familiarity with examining student work as part of the informal classroom observation experience, rich discussions will emerge. It is through these collaborative discussions that teaching and learning will become the focus of all efforts toward increased learning for both students and teachers. This book is not advocating that all postobservation conferences include examination of student work. The position is that the examination of student work should be incorporated into discussions as appropriate.

As the principal is out and about observing multiple teachers across grade levels and subject areas, more formalized professional development centering on student work might be worthy to consider. The principal has the vantage point of knowing what is being taught and how students are responding to learning. These insights about teaching and learning need to be shared in a way that invites teachers to consider the formal examination of student work as one way to inform instructional practices.

Looking Ahead ...

The tools used throughout this book are presented in the Appendix. The tools are blank so that the busy principal can reproduce them to collect data during informal classroom observations.

Appendix

CLASSROOM OBSERVATION TOOLS

Throughout each chapter, tools to assist the principal frame and conduct classroom observations are offered. Each tool presented in the chapters is provided as a blank form in this Appendix to help the busy principal collect usable and stable data during informal classroom observations.*

These tools are also available on Eye On Education's Web site as Adobe Acrobat PDF files. Those who have purchased this book have permission to download them and print them out. Instructions can be found on page v of this book.

---

*Unless indicated, all tools are from Zepeda (2007a, 2007b). Used with permission.

Tool 1: Assessing the Broad Characteristics of a Faculty

1. Number of teachers = _____   Male = ____   Female = ____

2. For each teacher, tally the number of years in teaching.
   Total number of years of experience = ____
   Average years of faculty experience = ____

3. Number of teachers whose experience falls within the following service ranges:
   a. 1–3 years = ____
   b. 4–7 years = ____
   c. 8–11 years = ____
   d. 12–15 years = ____
   e. 16–19 years = ____
   f. 20+ years = ____

4. Number of first-year teachers = ____

5. Number of teachers who will retire at the end of the year = ____

6. Wildcards:
   First-year teachers with experience = ____
   Alternatively certified teachers = ____
   Teachers returning to work after an extended leave = ____
   Other = ____

7. What overall patterns do you notice?

Tool 2: Tracking Informal Observations

Teacher	Observer	Informal Observations	Date of Follow-Up	Formal Observations	Period(s)/ Time(s)	Follow-up Topics

Tool 3: Focused Informal Classroom Observations

Teacher: _____

Date: _____

Administrator: _____

Class Period: 1 2 3 4 **5** 6 7 8

Common Classroom Expectations:

- Collaboration
- Differentiation
- Student Engagement
- Summarizing
- Display of Student Work
- Essential Question (EQ):

Expectations Domain	Presence = X
1. **Assessment:**	
2. **Nonverbal Representations:**	
3. **Modeling and Practice:**	
4. **Vocabulary:**	
5. **Summarizing:**	
6. **Collaboration:**	
7. **Student Goal Setting:**	
8. **Literacy:**	
9. **Problem-Solving:**	
10. **Questioning:**	
11. **Background Knowledge:**	
12. **Comparison and Contrast:**	
13. **Technology:**	

*Used with permission. Dr. Bill Kruskamp, principal, Creekland Middle School, Gwinnett County Public Schools (Lawrenceville, GA).

Tool 4:   Informal Classroom Observation: The Essential Question and Summarizing*

Teacher: _____

Date: _____

Essential Questions:

- ◆ Posted
- ◆ Guides Instruction
- ◆ Used at the end of lessons to assist summarizing and gather evidence of learning.

Summarizing:

- ◆ Reflects evidence of student learning
- ◆ All students participating
- ◆ Guided by the essential questions

What the students were doing?

_____

_____

_____

_____

Comments:

_____

_____

_____

_____

_____

---

*Used with permission. Dr. Bill Kruskamp, principal, Creekland Middle School, Gwinnett County Public Schools (Lawrenceville, GA).

Tool 5:   Selective Verbatim:
Praise, Correction, and Preventive Prompts*

Teacher: _____ Date of Observation: _____

Observer: _____

Class: _____ Period of the Day: _____

Time of Observation: Start: _____ End: _____

Total Time Spent in Observation: _____

Number of Students Present: _____ Grade level: _____

Topic of the Lesson: _____

Date of Postobservation Conference: _____

Teacher Comment/Response	Time	Praise	Correction	Preventive Prompt

*Developed by Theresa L. Benfante, Behavior Interventionist at Central Alternative School, Cobb County School District (Georgia). Used with permission.

Tool 6:   Open-Ended Classroom Observation Form*

Teacher's Name	Date	Beginning and Ending Times
Subject / Period	Grades	Location
Objectives to be observed. If none specified, write, "general."		Observer's Name

Times	*Observations*

*© National Association of Private Catholic and Independent Schools (2004). Used with permission.

Tool 7: Open-Ended—Key Areas

Teacher: _____ Date of Observation: _____

Observer: _____

Class: _____ Period of the Day: _____

Time of Observation: Start: _____ End: _____

Total Time Spent in Observation: _____

Number of Students Present: _____ Grade level: _____

Topic of the Lesson: _____

Date of Postobservation Conference: _____

I. Learning Objective:

II. Instructional Strategies (also note time):

III. Seating Arrangement:

IV. Transition Strategies:

V. Calling Patterns:

VI. Markers of Student Engagement:

Tool 8:   Sample Checklist Classroom Observation Form

Teacher: _____ Date of Observation: _____

Observer: _____

Class: _____ Period of the Day: _____

Time of Observation: Start: _____   End: _____

Total Time Spent in Observation: _____

Number of Students Present: _____   Grade level: _____

Topic of the Lesson: _____

Date of Postobservation Conference: _____

Students were
- ☐ working in small, cooperative groups
- ☐ making a presentation
- ☐ taking a test
- ☐ working independently at their desks
- ☐ viewing a film
- ☐ other _____

Teacher was
- ☐ lecturing
- ☐ facilitating a question and answer sequence
- ☐ working independently with students
- ☐ demonstrating a concept
- ☐ introducing a new concept
- ☐ reviewing for a test
- ☐ coming to closure
- ☐ other

Comments:

_____

_____

_____

_____

_____

_____

Tool 9: Mixed-Method Informal Classroom Observations— Informal Teacher Observation Form*

Teacher's Name: _____ Date of Observation:_____

Administrator: _____ Time: _____

Presence/ Absence	Criteria	Example Evidence
	1. Neat/well organized; safety information posted; Gotta Go Bag accessible	
	2. Artifacts—standards/curriculum-based, level appropriate, incorporate student work	
	3. Essential questions relating to lesson posted in an area for students to see	
	4. Classroom rules clearly posted with rewards/consequences	
	5. Transitions are appropriate and smooth	
	6. Routines and procedures are in place and followed	
	7. Students show engagement to current lesson or task	
	8. Mutual respect is evident	

Tool continues on next page.

*This tool was developed by Eric Ashton, principal, and Peggy Baggett, assistant principal of Daves Creek Elementary School, and Kathy Carpenter now principal at Riverwatch Middle School in Forsyth County Public Schools (GA). Used with permission.

Lesson Design and Delivery Incorporates the WOW* Design Qualities and Differentiation

Presence/ Absence	Criteria	Example Evidence
	9. Varied strategies and use of graphic organizers are used to meet needs of diverse learners— ESOL, EIP, special ed, and gifted	
	10. Student work is meaningful and has "real-life" application	
	11. Students are provided with specific and descriptive feedback throughout lesson to target areas of improvement	
	12. Varied levels of student work samples are posted for the purpose of student self-assessing against standards	
	13. Support for reading and math AIM goals is evident	
	14. Guided Reading Lessons: Small group reading purpose before and after Running reading records Genre Graphic organizers Questions/critical thinking	
	15. Variety of student grouping used to meet individual student needs	

Comments:

_____

_____

_____

_____

*WOW is "Working on the Work," a reform construct developed by Phil Schlechty (see *Shaking Up the Schoolhouse*, 2000).

Tool 10: Literacy Classroom Observation Checklist*

Teacher: _____ Date of Observation: _____ Observer: _____

Time of Observation: Start: ___ End: ___ Total Time Spent in Observation: ___

Number of Students Present: ___ Grade Level: ___ Topic of the Lesson: ___

Date of Postobservation Conference: _____

Literacy Block	Guided Reading	Well Organized Classroom	Literacy Rich Classroom
___ Read Aloud	___ Small Group area evident	___ Posts & uses rules, schedules, management system	___ Print-rich environment
___ Phonemic Awareness (K-2)	___ Uses appropriate narrative texts	___ Students routinely follow established rules & procedures	___ Concept charts
___ Concepts of Print (K-2)	___ Uses appropriate informational texts	___ Smooth transitions	___ Definition charts
___ Shared Reading	___ Differentiates instruction to meet all students' needs	___ Room organized, labeled	___ 6+1 Traits posters
___ Guided Reading	___ Uses before, during, after activities	___ Seating arranged for cooperative learning activities and interaction	___ Comprehension posters
___ Centers/Independent Work	___ Incorporates comprehension	___ Students accountable for learning	___ Authentic reading/writing observed
___ Monitored Independent Reading (MIR)	___ Incorporates fluency	___ Room clutter free, inviting	___ Student writing displayed
___ Explicit whole-class instruction	___ Teaches vocabulary of text	___ Productive, workable noise level	___ Classroom library evident, with narrative & informational texts in a wide variety of genres, leveled appropriately, for student use
___ Word Work	___ Listens to students read	___ Teacher has positive interaction with students	___ Leveled book boxes for MIR
___ Phonics/Spelling	___ Conducts running records	___ Positive interaction between students	___ Word Wall posted, consisting of general and content words
___ Comprehension	___ Has up-to-date records		
___ Fluency	___ Uses appropriate reading strategies (whisper, staggered, choral, paired, etc.) NO ROUND-ROBIN reading!		
___ Oral Language			
___ Interactive/Shared Writing			
___ Modeled Writing			
___ Directed Writing			
___ 6+1 Traits of Writing			
___ Writer's Workshop			
___ Independent Writing			

Tool continues on next page.

Centers/Independent Work	Explicit Instruction	Writing	MIR
__ Management system in place __ Students responsible for learning __ Engaging activities __ Authentic reading/writing activities __ Student accountability system __ Differentiated work matches student needs __ Work reinforces previously taught concepts	__ Grade-Level teacher talk __ Shared Reading- all students __ Uses Houghton Mifflin for shared reading __ Other grade-level texts (Big Books, poetry, informational) __ All students have access to text __ Book Talk __ Preteaches vocabulary __ Use comprehension strategies before, during, after activities __ Interactive, hands-on activities __ Integrated content core __ Incorporates good ESL strategies	__ Writing Process __ Mini Lesson __ 6+1 Traits of Writing __ Student Accountability/status of class __ Interactive/shared writing (K-2) __ Modeled Writing __ Directed Writing __ Independent Writing __ Student published writing available to other students __ Writing area & materials evident	__ Minimum 15-20 minutes per day __ Students self-select books from independent reading level-interest based books provided by teacher __ Variety of genres provided __ Monitoring, nongraded (student reflections, cooperative learning discussions, conferences, bookmarks, journals, pictures, etc.)

Word Work	Assessment	Collaboration	Curriculum Mapping
__ Phonemic Awareness (K-2) __ Phonics __ Vocabulary __ Differentiated Spelling __ Grade-level Language Arts __ Word Wall posted __ Word Wall systematically used in instruction	__ Keeps up-to-date running records with guided reading levels __ Submits guided reading levels as requested __ Maintains detailed formal and informal assessment records __ Maintains list of below level students	__ Collaborates with team in analyzing assessment data __ Collaboratively plans for/provides interventions, reteaching, enrichment, differentiation	__ Creates curriculum map, based on Utah State Core and student needs __ Uses curriculum map to guide instruction

*This tool was developed by the Jordan School District, Sandy, UT. Acknowledgement is given to Dana L. Bickmore, executive director for curriculum and staff development and Kathy Ridd, elementary language arts and early childhood consultant of the Jordan School District. Used with permission.

Tool 11: Anecdotal and Checklist Data-Collection Method, Focus on Cooperative Learning

Teacher: _____ Date of Observation: _____

Observer: _____

Class: _____ Period of the Day: _____

Time of Observation: Start: _____ End: _____

Total Time Spent in Observation: _____

Number of Students Present: _____ Grade level: _____

Topic of the Lesson: _____

Date of Postobservation Conference: _____

Focus	Presence = X or Absence = 0	Notes
Objectives for the cooperative learning group		
Clarity of directions		
Movement into groups		
Monitoring and intervening strategies		
Interaction with students		
Follow-up instruction		

Tool 12:   Foreign Language Observation Checklist*

Teacher: _____   Date of Observation: _____

Observer: _____

Class: _____   Period of the Day: _____

Time of Observation: Start: _____   End: _____

Total Time Spent in Observation: _____

Number of Students Present: _____   Grade level: _____

Topic of the Lesson: _____

Date of Postobservation Conference: _____

1. Are all language modalities evident in the lesson (speaking, writing, listening, and reading)?

2. Is culture evident in the lesson?

3. Does the teacher use a wide variety of prepared and authentic materials at appropriate levels?

4. Is the purpose of each activity clearly explained to the students?

5. Does the teacher model activities when giving directions and check for comprehension afterward?

6. Are the transitions between activities smooth?

7. Are the students on task and actively involved in the learning process?

8. Is there an appropriate use of partner–pair or small group activities?

---

*Developed by Marcia Wilbur, PhD, executive director, Curriculum and Content Development for the Advanced Placement Program at the College Board, based on her work at Gull Lake High School Foreign Language Department, Richland, Michigan. Used with permission.

Tool 13: Sample Seating Chart

Teacher: _____ Date of Observation: _____

Observer: _____

Class: _____ Period of the Day: _____

Time of Observation: Start: _____ End: _____

Total Time Spent in Observation: _____

Number of Students Present: _____ Grade level: _____

Topic of the Lesson: _____

Date of Postobservation Conference: _____

Draw Seating Chart here:

Tool 14: Synchronous Clinical Observation Music Tool*

---

*The Synchronous Clinical Observation Music Tool was developed by Kevin Shorner-Johnson, a doctoral candidate in the Music Education Department at the University of Georgia. Used with permission.

Tool 15: Observation Guide Using Bloom's Taxonomy

Teacher: _____ Date of Observation: _____

Observer: _____

Class: _____ Period of the Day: _____

Time of Observation: Start: _____   End: _____

Total Time Spent in Observation: _____

Number of Students Present: _____   Grade level: _____

Topic of the Lesson: _____

Date of Postobservation Conference: _____

		Levels of Thinking					
Time	*Questions and Activities*	*K N O W L E D G E*	*C O M P R E H E N S I O N*	*A P P L I C A T I O N*	*A N A L Y S I S*	*S Y N T H E S I S*	*E V A L U A T I O N*

Tool 16: Alternative Observation Guide Using Bloom's Taxonomy

Teacher: _____   Date of Observation: _____

Observer: _____

Class: _____   Period of the Day: _____

Time of Observation: Start: _____   End: _____

Total Time Spent in Observation: _____

Number of Students Present: _____   Grade level: _____

Topic of the Lesson: _____

Date of Postobservation Conference: _____

Time	Teacher Questions	Taxonomy Level

Tool 17: Focus on Wait Time

Teacher: _____ Date of Observation: _____

Observer: _____

Class: _____ Period of the Day: _____

Time of Observation: Start: _____ End: _____

Total Time Spent in Observation: _____

Number of Students Present: _____ Grade level: _____

Topic of the Lesson: _____

Date of Postobservation Conference: _____

Teacher Question	*Wait Time* *(Seconds)*

Tool 18: Wait Time With Bloom's Taxonomy for Examining Levels of Questions

Teacher: _____ Date of Observation: _____

Observer: _____

Class: _____ Period of the Day: _____

Time of Observation: Start: _____ End: _____

Total Time Spent in Observation: _____

Number of Students Present: _____ Grade level: _____

Topic of the Lesson: _____

Date of Postobservation Conference: _____

Teacher Question	Wait Time (Seconds)	Question Domain

Tool 19: Tracking Calling Patterns

Teacher: _____ Date of Observation: _____

Observer: _____

Class: _____ Period of the Day: _____

Time of Observation: Start: _____ End: _____

Total Time Spent in Observation: _____

Number of Students Present: _____ Grade level: _____

Topic of the Lesson: _____

Date of Postobservation Conference: _____

Legend:

- ♦ Entire Class Response—ECR
- ♦ Individual Response—IR
- ♦ Individual Help—IH
- ♦ Question—Q
- ♦ Comment—C

Front of Room

	A	B	C	D
1.				
2.				
3.				
4.				
5.				

Tool 20:   Tracking Calling Patterns—Seating Chart*

Teacher: _____   Date of Observation: _____

Observer: _____

Class: _____   Period of the Day: _____

Time of Observation: Start: _____   End: _____

Total Time Spent in Observation: _____

Number of Students Present: _____   Grade level: _____

Topic of the Lesson: _____

Date of Postobservation Conference: _____

_____

*This tool was developed by Meredith A. Byrd, Clayton County Public Schools (Jonesboro, GA).

Tool 21: Cause and Effect

Teacher: _____ Date of Observation: _____

Observer: _____

Class: _____ Period of the Day: _____

Time of Observation: Start: _____   End: _____

Total Time Spent in Observation: _____

Number of Students Present: _____ Grade level: _____

Topic of the Lesson: _____

Date of Postobservation Conference: _____

Time	*Teacher*	*Student Response or Activity*

Tool 22: Variety of Instructional Materials

Teacher: _____ Date of Observation: _____

Observer: _____

Class: _____ Period of the Day: _____

Time of Observation: Start: _____ End: _____

Total Time Spent in Observation: _____

Number of Students Present: _____ Grade level: _____

Topic of the Lesson: _____

Date of Postobservation Conference: _____

Time	Instructional Method	Teacher Behavior	Student Activities

Tool 23: Examining Teacher–Student Discussion With a Focus on How Student Comments Are Incorporated Into the Lesson

Teacher: _____ Date of Observation: _____

Observer: _____

Class: _____ Period of the Day: _____

Time of Observation: Start: _____ End: _____

Total Time Spent in Observation: _____

Number of Students Present: _____ Grade level: _____

Topic of the Lesson: _____

Date of Postobservation Conference: _____

Time	Teacher Talk/Question	Student Response	How Student Comments Are Used

Tool 24: Focus on Tracking Transition Patterns

Teacher: _____ Date of Observation: _____

Observer: _____

Class: _____ Period of the Day: _____

Time of Observation: Start: _____ End: _____

Total Time Spent in Observation: _____

Number of Students Present: _____ Grade level: _____

Topic of the Lesson: _____

Date of Postobservation Conference: _____

Instruction/Activity	Transition	Student Response

Tool 25:   Tracking Student Behavior

Teacher: _____ Date of Observation: _____

Observer: _____

Class: _____ Period of the Day: _____

Time of Observation: Start: _____   End: _____

Total Time Spent in Observation: _____

Number of Students Present: _____ Grade level: _____

Topic of the Lesson: _____

Date of Postobservation Conference: _____

	Teacher	*&*	*Student*

Tool 26: Classroom Traffic—Seating Chart

Teacher: _____ Date of Observation: _____

Observer: _____

Class: _____ Period of the Day: _____

Time of Observation: Start: _____ End: _____

Total Time Spent in Observation: _____

Number of Students Present: _____ Grade level: _____

Topic of the Lesson: _____

Date of Postobservation Conference: _____

Board

Tool 27: Beginning of Class Routines

Teacher: _____ Date of Observation: _____

Observer: _____

Class: _____ Period of the Day: _____

Time of Observation: Start: _____ End: _____

Total Time Spent in Observation: _____

Number of Students Present: _____ Grade level: _____

Topic of the Lesson: _____

Date of Postobservation Conference: _____

	Beginning of the Period	*Student Behavior*

Tool 28: Tracking End of Class Routines

Teacher: _____ Date of Observation: _____

Observer: _____

Class: _____ Period of the Day: _____

Time of Observation: Start: _____   End: _____

Total Time Spent in Observation: _____

Number of Students Present: _____   Grade level: _____

Topic of the Lesson: _____

Date of Postobservation Conference: _____

	Ending of the Period	*Student Behavior*

Tool 29:   Focus on Cooperative Learning

Focus	*Notes*
Objectives for the cooperative learning group	
Clarity of directions	
Transitions from small to large group work	
Monitoring and intervening strategies	
Evaluation strategies	
Interactions with students	
Follow-up instruction	

Tool 30: Cooperative Learning—
Student Interactions and Teacher Monitoring

Teacher: _____ Date of Observation: _____

Observer: _____

Class: _____ Period of the Day: _____

Time of Observation: Start: _____ End: _____

Total Time Spent in Observation: _____

Number of Students Present: _____ Grade level: _____

Topic of the Lesson: _____

Date of Postobservation Conference: _____

Group	Number in Group	Student Interaction	Teacher Monitoring Strategies

Tool 31: Tracking Teacher Behaviors Promoting Cooperative Learning

Teacher: _____ Date of Observation: _____

Observer: _____

Class: _____ Period of the Day: _____

Time of Observation: Start: _____ End: _____

Total Time Spent in Observation: _____

Number of Students Present: _____ Grade level: _____

Topic of the Lesson: _____

Date of Postobservation Conference: _____

Focus on Cooperative Learning	Presence or Absence	Notes
Objectives for the cooperative learning group		
Clarity of directions		
Movement into groups		
Monitoring and intervening strategies		
Evaluation Strategies		
Interaction with students		
Follow-up instruction—large-group processing		

Tool 32: Classroom Observation Guide to Track Technology Integration*

Teacher: _____ Date of Observation: _____

Observer: _____

Class: _____ Period of the Day: _____

Time of Observation: Start: _____ End: _____

Total Time Spent in Observation: _____

Number of Students Present: _____ Grade level: _____

Topic of the Lesson: _____

Date of Postobservation Conference: _____

Indicators for Technology Integration

Rate each of the following using this rating scale:

1 = *Little* evidence of technology use.

2 = *Some* evidence that technology is used in limited amounts and with simple tasks—more productivity oriented.

3 = Evidence that teacher *uses* technology and provides assistance to students with spreadsheets, word processing, demonstrations.

4 = Teacher is *comfortable* with technology use. A *variety* of technology is used daily, and technology is an integral part of classroom instruction.

5 = Not applicable to the lesson.

_____

_____ 1. **Students use computers for drill and practice activities; use of stand-alone computer software.**

   ♦ Use of networkable programs such as Accelerated Reader and Accelerated Math

   ♦ Use of instructional Web-based software such as Riverdeep

_____ 2. **Students use computers for instructional purposes.**

   ♦ Use of computers for performance assessments—such as, PowerPoint, Excel, and so forth

   ♦ Use of computers for Web-based research using computers to gather data

Tool continues on next page.

Tool 32:   Classroom Observation Guide to Track Technology Integration (Cont'd)

♦ Using a combination of software and Web-based research to analyze data and draw conclusions

♦ Taking data and conclusions and presenting it using some type of multimedia presentation

____ 3. Teacher uses presentation software such as PowerPoint during instruction.

____ 4. Teacher uses projection tools during instruction.

♦ Uses overhead projector

♦ Uses multimedia projector

♦ Uses multimedia projector with VCR

♦ Uses multimedia projector with SmartBoard or ActivBoard

____ 5. Teacher incorporates the use of other devices during instruction.

♦ Digital camera

♦ Scanner

♦ iPod

♦ Graphing calculators

____ 6. Teacher incorporates technology within the lesson, and student work is indicative of seamless transitions between traditional instruction and technology integration.

Classroom Observation Running Notes:

The Classroom Observation Guide to Track Technology Integration Tool was developed by Ann G. Haughey as part of her coursework in supervision theory and her problem of practice while working toward her specialist in education degree at the University of Georgia. Ann G. Haughey is the technology coordinator for Wilkes County Schools (Washington, GA).

Tool 33: Running Notes With a Timeline

Teacher: _____ Date of Observation: _____

Observer: _____

Class: _____ Period of the Day: _____

Time of Observation: Start: _____   End: _____

Total Time Spent in Observation: _____

Number of Students Present: _____   Grade level: _____

Topic of the Lesson: _____

Date of Postobservation Conference: _____

Time	Running Notes

Tool 34: Sample Informal Postobservation Feedback Form

Teacher: _____ Date of Observation: _____

Observer: _____

Class: _____ Period of the Day: _____

Time of Observation: Start: _____ End: _____

Total Time Spent in Observation: _____

Number of Students Present: _____ Grade level: _____

Topic of the Lesson: _____

Date of Postobservation Conference: _____

Students were

- ☐ working in small, cooperative groups
- ☐ making a presentation
- ☐ taking a test
- ☐ working independently at their desks
- ☐ viewing a film
- ☐ other: Pair-share groups to practice telling time in Spanish

Teacher was

- ☐ lecturing
- ☐ facilitating a question and answer sequence
- ☐ working independently with students
- ☐ demonstrating a concept
- ☐ introducing a new concept
- ☐ reviewing for a test
- ☐ coming to closure
- ☐ other

Comments:

_____

_____

_____

_____

Tool 35:   Presentation of Postobservation Conference Notes

Teacher: _____ Date of Observation: _____

Observer: _____

Class: _____ Period of the Day: _____

Time of Observation: Start: _____ End: _____

Total Time Spent in Observation: _____

Number of Students Present: _____ Grade level: _____

Topic of the Lesson: _____

Date of Postobservation Conference: _____

Time	Running Notes	Teacher Questions

Tool 36:   Tracking Sheet—Faculty Needs

Teacher: _____ Years: 2008 to _____

Years at School = _____

Short-Term Instructional Goal(s): _____

Long-Term Instructional Goal(s): _____

Log of Informal Observations

Observation Date: _____
Follow-up:

Observation Date: _____
Follow-up:

Tool 37:   Questions to Lead the
Teacher Talk About Student-Generated Artifacts

1. What information about student learning have you gleaned from the student thoughts and proofs from the cards?

2. Do the cards later get used so students can write an essay?

3. Today, what will you do to review the proofs and the cards with students?

4. What do these artifacts tell you about what you are teaching and why?

5. If you could rework the lesson from yesterday, what would you do differently and why?

6. How can this lesson and in-class assignment be modified based on the patterns found in these cards and the proofs?

Tool 38:   Thinking, Listening and Reflecting
With Colleagues About Student Work*

Reflecting on the process

Looking for evidence of student thinking ...

+ What did you see in this student's work that was interesting or surprising?

+ What did you learn about how this student thinks and learns?

+ What about the process helped you to see and learn these things?

Reflecting on one's own thinking ...

+ What questions about teaching and assessment did looking at the students' work raise for you?

+ How can you pursue these questions further?

+ Are there things you would like to try in your classroom as a result of looking at this student's work?

Source: *Copyright 2007 ATLAS Learning Communities. Adapted and used with permission.

Tool 39: Examining Student Work by Content Standards

Teacher: _____ Date of Observation: _____

Observer: _____

Class: _____ Period of the Day: _____

Time of Observation: Start: _____ End: _____

Total Time Spent in Observation: _____

Number of Students Present: _____ Grade level: _____

Topic of the Lesson: _____

Date of Postobservation Conference: _____

Artifact:

Narrative Analysis of Grade-Level-Appropriate Text

Writing Strategies

Organization and Focus

Research and Technology

Questions to Guide the Examination and Discussion of ...

Tool 40: Planning Guide—What Next?

1. What content needs to be reviewed or retaught based on the discussion during the postobservation conference?

2. What instructional strategies would most likely help move learning forward to meet goals and objectives?

3. What materials are needed?

References

Acheson, K. A., & Gall, M. D. (1997). *Techniques in the clinical supervision of teachers: Preservice and inservice applications* (4th ed.). White Plains, NY: Longman.

ATLAS Learning Communities, Inc. (2007). *ATLAS—Learning from student work*. Cambridge, MA: Author.

Bellon, J. J., & Bellon, E. C. (1982). *Classroom supervision and instructional improvement: A synergetic process* (2nd ed.). Dubuque, IA: Kendall/Hunt.

Blasé, J. R., & Blasé, J. J. (1998). *Handbook of instructional leadership: How really good principals promote teaching and learning*. Thousand Oaks, CA: Corwin. Press.

Bloom, B. S. (Ed.). (1956). *Taxonomy of educational objectives: The classification of educational goals*. New York: Longman.

Brookfield, S. D. (1986). *Understanding and facilitating adult learning: A comprehensive analysis of principles and effective practices*. San Francisco: Jossey-Bass.

Burden, P. (1982, February). *Developmental supervision: Reducing teacher stress at different career stages*. Paper presented at the Association of Teacher Educators National Conference, Phoenix, AZ.

Burke, P. J., Christensen, J. C., & Fessler, R. (1984). *Teacher career stages: Implications for staff development*. Bloomington, IN: Phi Delta Kappa Educational Foundation.

Center for Comprehensive School Reform and Improvement. (2007). *Using the classroom walk-through as an instructional leadership strategy*. Washington DC: Learning Point Associates. Author.

Christensen, J. P., Burke, P. J., Fessler, R., & Hagstrom, D. (1983). *Stages of teachers' careers: Implications for professional development*. Washington, DC: National Institute of Education. (ERIC Document Reproduction Service No. ED227054)

Downey, C. J., Steffy, B. E., English, F. W., Frase, L. E., & Poston, W. K., Jr. (2004). *Changing school supervisory practices one teacher at a time: The three-minute classroom walk-through*. Thousand Oaks, CA: Corwin.

Feiman, S., & Floden, R. (1980). *What's all this talk about teacher development?* East Lansing, MI: Institute for Research on Teaching. (ERIC Document Reproduction Service No. ED189088)

FutureCents. (n.d.). *Twelve guidelines for managing by walking around (MB WA)*. Retrieved February 14, 2005, from www.futruecents.com/ mainmbwa.htm

Gagné, R. M., Briggs, L. J., & Wager, W. W. (1992). *Principles of instructional design* (4th ed.). Fort Worth, TX: Harcourt Brace College.

Huberman, M. (1993). *The lives of teachers* (J. Neufeld, Trans.). New York: Teachers College Press.

Johnson, D. W., & Johnson, R. T. (1994). Learning together. In S. Sharan (Ed.), *Handbook of cooperative learning methods* (pp. 51–65). Westport, CT: Greenwood Press.

Katz, L. (1972). Developmental stages of preschool teachers. *Elementary School Journal, 73(1)*, 50–54.

Knowles, M. S. (1980). *The modern practice of adult education: From pedagogy to andragogy* (2nd ed.). Chicago: Follett.

Kurtoglu-Hooton, N. (2004, July). Postobservation feedback as an instigator of teacher learning and change. *International Association of Teachers of English as a Foreign Language TTED SIG E-Newsletter*. Retrieved February 28, 2005, from www.ihes.com/ttsig/resources/e-newsletter/FreatureArticles.pdf

Manning, R. C. (1988). *The teacher evaluation handbook: Step-by-step techniques and forms for improving instruction.* Paramus, NJ: Prentice Hall.

McDonald, J. (2001). Students' work and teachers' learning. In A. Lieberman & L. Miller (Eds.), *Teachers caught in the action: Professional development that matters* (pp. 209–235). New York: Teachers College Press.

McGreal, T. L. (1983). *Effective teacher evaluation.* Alexandria, VA: Association for Supervision and Curriculum Development.

McGreal, T. L. (1988). Evaluation for enhancing instruction: Linking teacher evaluation and staff development. In S. J. Stanley & W. J. Popham (Eds.), *Teacher evaluation: Six prescriptions for success* (pp. 1–29). Alexandria, VA: Association for Supervision and Curriculum Development.

National Education Association Foundation for the Improvement of Education. (2003). *Using data about classroom practice and student work to improve professional development for educators.* Washington, DC: Author.

Northwest Regional Educational Laboratory. (n.d.). *Overview of technology integration in schools.* Portland, OR: Author. Retrieved April 7, 2008 from http://www.netc.org/images/pdf/tech.integration.pdf

Peters, T. J., & Waterman, R. H., Jr. (1982). *In search of excellence: Lessons from America's best run companies.* New York: Harper & Row.

Rowe, M. B. (1986). Wait time: Slowing down may be a way of speeding up. *Journal of Teacher Education, 37(1),* 43–50.

Schlechty, P. (2000). *Shaking up the schoolhouse.* San Francisco: Jossey-Bass.

Sparks, D., & Hirsh, S. (1997). *A new vision for staff development.* Oxford, OH: National Staff Development Council.

Stahl, R. J. (1994). *Using "think-time" and "wait-time" skillfully in the class-room.* Bloomington, IN: ERIC Clearinghouse for Social Studies/Social Science Education. Retrieved February 25, 2005, from http://atozteacherstuff.com/ pages/1884.shtml

Tomlinson, C. A. (1999). *The differentiated classroom: Responding to the needs of all learners.* Alexandria, VA: Association for Supervision and Curriculum Development.

Wang, C. M., & Ong, G. (2003). *Questioning techniques for active learning. Ideas on teaching.* Retrieved June 12, 2008, from http://www.cdtl.nus.edu.sg/ideas/iot2.htm

Wood, F. H., & Killian, J. E. (1998). Job-embedded learning makes the difference in school improvement. *Journal of Staff Development, 19(1),* 52-54.

Zepeda. S. J. (2007a). *The principal as instructional leader: A handbook for supervisors* (2nd ed.). Larchmont, NY: Eye on Education.

Zepeda, S. J. (2007b). *Instructional supervision: Applying tools and concepts* (2nd ed.). Larchmont, NY: Eye on Education.

Zepeda, S. J. (2008). *Professional development: What works.* Larchmont, NY: Eye on Education.